POLITICAL PATHOLOGIES FROM *THE SOPRANOS* TO *SUCCESSION*

Political Pathologies from The Sopranos *to* Succession argues that highly praised prestige TV shows reveal the underlying fantasies and contradictions of upper-middle-class political centrists.

Through a psychoanalytic interpretation of *The Sopranos, Breaking Bad, The Wire, House of Cards, Dexter, Game of Thrones*, and *Succession*, Robert Samuels uncovers how moderate "liberals" have helped to produce and maintain the libertarian Right. Samuels' analysis explores the difference between contemporary centrists and the foundations of liberal democracy, exposing the myth of the "liberal media" and considers the consequences of these celebrated series, including the undermining of trust in modern liberal democratic institutions. *Political Pathologies from* The Sopranos *to* Succession contributes to a greater understanding of the ways media and political ideology can circulate on a global level through the psychopathology of class consciousness.

This book will be of great interest to academics and scholars considering intersections of psychoanalytic studies, television studies, and politics.

Robert Samuels, PhD, holds doctorates in Psychoanalysis and English and teaches at the University of California, Santa Barbara, USA.

POLITICAL PATHOLOGIES FROM *THE SOPRANOS* TO *SUCCESSION*

Prestige TV and the Contradictions of the "Liberal" Class

Robert Samuels

Routledge
Taylor & Francis Group
LONDON AND NEW YORK

Designed cover image: Getty

First published 2023
by Routledge
4 Park Square, Milton Park, Abingdon, Oxon OX14 4RN

and by Routledge
605 Third Avenue, New York, NY 10158

Routledge is an imprint of the Taylor & Francis Group, an informa business

© 2023 Robert Samuels

The right of Robert Samuels to be identified as author of this work has been asserted in accordance with sections 77 and 78 of the Copyright, Designs and Patents Act 1988.

All rights reserved. No part of this book may be reprinted or reproduced or utilised in any form or by any electronic, mechanical, or other means, now known or hereafter invented, including photocopying and recording, or in any information storage or retrieval system, without permission in writing from the publishers.

Trademark notice: Product or corporate names may be trademarks or registered trademarks, and are used only for identification and explanation without intent to infringe.

British Library Cataloguing-in-Publication Data
A catalogue record for this book is available from the British Library

ISBN: 978-1-032-40340-3 (hbk)
ISBN: 978-1-032-40339-7 (pbk)
ISBN: 978-1-003-35260-0 (ebk)

DOI: 10.4324/9781003352600

Typeset in Bembo
by KnowledgeWorks Global Ltd.

CONTENTS

1	Introduction	1
2	*The Sopranos:* Make TV Elite Again	13
3	*Breaking Bad:* From Walter White to the Alt-Right	29
4	*The Wire* and the Death of Liberal Institutions	42
5	*House of Cards* and the Fall of the Liberal Class	55
6	*Dexter:* Artistic Violence as Class Distinction	74
7	*Game of Thrones:* Climate Change, Gender Wars, and the Fictionalized Past	89
8	Conclusion: *Succession* and the Metafictional Political Present	103
	Index	*117*

1

INTRODUCTION

The central argument of this book is that highly praised prestige TV shows reveal the underlying psychology of upper-middle class liberals.[1] Through a psycho-analytic interpretation of *The Sopranos, Breaking Bad, The Wire, House of Cards, Dexter, Game of Thrones*, and *Succession*, I reveal how moderates are shaped by their need to signal their excellence and goodness by consuming high-status cultural objects. Similar to the way that higher education is used to produce and maintain class dominance through selective admissions processes, the consumption of elite TV shows represents not only an idealization of a particular type of culture but, more importantly, the form and content of these programs define itself against TV for the masses.[2] For instance, when HBO declares it is not TV, it is playing on a clear division between elite culture and the degraded mass culture. As Pierre Bourdieu has taught us, prestige is always generated from exclusivity and social hierarchy, and in the case of prestige TV, the targeting of high-income consumers who can pay for expensive subscriptions requires producing a discourse around an idealized artistic form.[3]

While the prestige shows examined in this book derive from a particular culture and time period, due to the role played by online streaming services, their influence is able to transcend older temporal and spatial limitations.[4] As products of a globalizing cultural process, a new mode of elite cultural aesthetics spreads throughout the world, and even if many of the new viewers do not come from the upper-middle class or from the United States, the audience is still affected by the psychopathology and unconscious ideology of these shows. As Marx insisted, the ruling ideas of a society derive from the ruling class, and in our cultural period, it is the upper 9.9% of income earners who represent the ruling class. What I seek to elaborate is the underlying psychopathology shaping elite professionals and political centrists.

Although much of my analysis of prestige TV is derived from Michael Newman's and Elana Levine's *Legitimating Television*, what I add is the use of

DOI: 10.4324/9781003352600-1

2 Introduction

psychoanalysis to understand the subjectivity of contemporary upper-middle class citizens, which helps to define both their politics and their media consumption habits.[5] On the most basic level, this class is shaped by a desire to be seen as morally good in a society of extreme inequality. While they may identify as liberals, their selfish pursuit of privilege, power, and profit coupled with constant virtue signaling results in an undermining of liberal democratic institutions.[6] As Chris Hedges argues in his *Death of the Liberal Class*, universities, journalistic institutions, and the Democratic party have all been undermined from within by the same drive of selfish careerism.[7] From this perspective, it is often so-called liberals who have harmed liberal institutions from within, and in the case of the "liberal media," we find the same unacknowledged process. For instance, when the head of CBS, Les Moonves, said that "Donald Trump may not be good for America, but he is damn good for CBS," he revealed the underlying force of capitalist greed in contemporary mass media.[8] As we shall see, this amoral capitalistic drive is at the center of many prestige TV series; however, the twist is that selfish greed is both celebrated and condemned in an obsessional narcissistic fashion.

Since contemporary moderate liberals want to see themselves as good people with good intentions, they have to repress their own anti-social desires, and one way that they do this is by projecting their drives onto others who they then both identify with and condemn from a distance.[9] Thus, when scholars argue that a defining aspect of prestige TV shows is that they have morally complex lead characters, what they are often pointing to is the way that these cultural objects provide the audience with an opportunity to both live out fantasies of selfish greed and enjoyment while also condemning these desires from a distance. For example, Tony Soprano not only acts on his violent urges and sexual compulsions, but he also goes to therapy to discuss some of the ramifications of his actions. In short, Tony is an ambivalent, divided character catering to an internally divided audience.

Key artistic devices that help to enable this process of identification and moral condemnation are the use of irony, metafiction, and aesthetic form.[10] In fact, what often signals the artistic pretensions of these shows is their use of strange camera angles, reflected images, and saturated colors. These non-functional devices signal to the audience that they are watching carefully thought-out art, which is not focused purely on trying to depict reality. As Bourdieu insists, this separation from reference has a class-based dimension because it is only the upper class that has the freedom, time, and resources to indulge in pure artistic contemplation.[11] The upper-middle class then can signal their elite status by spending time and money on activities that serve no direct function, while the working class consumes culture that reflects their own focus on necessity and referentiality.

The use of pure aesthetic form also helps to create distance between what is being watched and the viewer's own sense of identity. For example, when Frank Underwood directly addresses the audience in *House of Cards*, the program sets up a doubled reality where the plot is developed at the same time that the fictional status of the series is highlighted. This split, ironic representation enables the audience to both identify with Underwood's destructive careerism and condemn his selfish actions. Since the liberal audiences want to believe in their own moral goodness, they have to repress and project their own anti-social desires, and as Freud said in relation to obsessive-compulsive neurotics, they are repulsed by what attracts them, and attracted to what repulses them.[12]

Even though streaming has allowed many of these elite shows to reach a wider, global audience, their aesthetics and content are shaped by centrist, upper-middle class psychology. Moreover, this communication between the productions and the audience occurs on a mostly unconscious level, and so both the producers and viewers of these shows are not aware of the underlying psychopathology. My approach, then, goes against the cultural studies' argument that the audiences are not dupes of the media they consume; instead, I argue that psychoanalysis pushes us to affirm that the real meaning and effect of these productions is often repressed and unacknowledged, and that is one reason why we need cultural critics to interpret the hidden structures and meanings. On the most basic level, obsessional narcissists seek to maintain a positive self-image by repressing their transgressive anti-social fantasies and projecting their ambivalent desires into the safe realm of fantasy and popular culture. While some would argue that this process can lead to insight, psychoanalysis tells us that the only way to discover the truth of our desires and fears is to engage in the process of tracing the repressed association and feelings connected to the material.

The Political Pathology of the Upper-Middle Class

One reason why it is important to understand prestige TV and its relation to the psychopathologies of the upper-middle class is that this group shapes and controls most of the major social institutions in liberal democracies. As Matthew Stewart documents in his *The 9.9%*, education, real estate, political parties, and parenting have been restructured by the interests of these high earners.[13] This group strives to be at the very top and fears falling into the working class, and so they try to enhance their social status by making every institution work in their favor. Not only do they want to live in the "best" neighborhoods with the "best" schools, but these meritocratic elites seek to spend excessive resources on ensuring that their children end up going to the top universities. Their constant focus on what society deems to be the best also reflects on their consumer habits, and in the case of media consumption, their knowledge of prestige TV shows helps them to produce a sense of belonging to the elite as they separate themselves from the non-elites.

There is thus a perfect marriage between the media corporations seeking out people who will pay premium subscriptions for prestige TV and a social class seeking to maintain and signal its elite status. Moreover, an underlying message that we find circulating in many of these programs is that the only solution to an unequal capitalistic society is to focus on protecting the interests of yourself and those closest to you.[14] Just as Tony Soprano and Walter White rationalize

4 Introduction

their destructive greed by arguing that they are just trying to provide for their family, the upper-middle class elites justify their selfish pursuits by taking on a survivalist mentality: In a society that only benefits a select few, one has to focus on one's own interests.[15] Furthermore, any guilt and shame that is generated from being aware of this combination of inequality and selfish greed can be repressed and contained by turning to the depiction of destructive desires in fictional representations.

In terms of contemporary politics, it is vital to see how upper-middle class centrists have helped to produce the reactionary Right. As many have pointed out, one of the main reasons for the rise of Right-wing politics is the failure of liberal parties to help the working class.[16] Due in part to the dominant influence of the upper-middle class, centrists have become less concerned with unions, workers' rights, and economic inequality as they focus on education as the key to economic justice; however, institutions of education have become highly stratified and unequal, and so they function on average to decrease social mobility.[17] Although liberal politicians should know that their preferred policies have not worked, they are so invested in seeing themselves as morally good that they simply repress the destructive effects of their actions.[18]

Another way that centrist liberals have contributed to Right-wing politics is through the constant media depiction of failed liberal social institutions coupled with the focus on individuals who take matters into their own hands. In many of the prestige TV shows examined in this book, we see how the failure of politicians, courts, police, educators, and healthcare providers pushes the hero to go outside the law and social system. While the liberal centrist audience may ultimately condemn the actions of the anti-social criminal, we also find an underlying identification with the individual who seeks out their own freedom and justice. As an example of libertarian ideology, the male anti-heroes of these programs pursue their own self-interest at the cost of everyone else around them.

Not only are these shows dominated by men, but they also tend to depict women as nagging moralists seeking to contain the freedom and desire of their male counterparts.[19] For example, Tony Soprano is harassed by his mother, his wife, and female psychiatrist as he seeks to provide for his family and satisfy his compulsions.[20] Likewise, *Breaking Bad*'s Walter White gains the audience's sympathy as his wife is attacked for not being more supportive of his illegal activities. Even a show like *Game of Thrones*, which appears to depict the rise in power of women ends up demonizing females for their violent reaction to masculine privilege.[21] What may be happening here is that liberal centrists want to believe that our society is becoming more just and equal, but on some level, they still desire to hold onto their power and privilege.

As we shall see in our examination of *The Wire*, the failure of liberal institutions is coupled with a liberal mode of racism where people of color are both idealized and debased for their violence and sexuality.[22] Since liberals do not want to admit that they may have racist beliefs, they tend to idealize people of color at the same time they condemn them for their uncivilized behavior. On one level, we find the fantasy that certain groups of people are able to live more freely because they are less controlled by the dictates of society, and on another level, we find the dominant class vicariously enjoying the sex and violence of the unrepressed minority group at a distance. In the form of cultural slumming, the white upper-middle class finds enjoyment in watching the depiction of the imagined actions of "uncivilized" groups.[23] Moreover, even if shows like *The Wire* are consumed now by a non-elite and non-white audience, these series are still shaped by the underlying values and pathologies of the writers and directors.

It is important to stress that TV tends to focus on the individual even when it is dealing with systemic issues like race, class, and gender hierarchies. As a way of solidifying emotional connections between the audience and the main characters of a show, it is necessary to highlight the actions of the individual, and this type of focus feeds into the individualistic mentality of the liberal upper-middle class. Even though they might pay lip service to systemic issues, liberal elites ultimately believe that it is up to the individual to sink or swim on their own.[24] Criminal anti-heroes are, in a sense, only an exaggerated form of this hyper-individualistic liberal philosophy. Furthermore, since the audience is watching criminals, they can take a distance from their own anti-social greed and transgressive compulsions.

The liberal fascination with criminality and anti-social behavior is related to the centrists' obsession with a politician like Donald Trump. As someone who positions himself against political correctness and identity politics, Trump embodies many of the characteristics of Tony Soprano, and while the liberal audience may denounce Tony's and Trump's words and actions, they feed a media system that gives the people what they want, and what they want is to watch anti-social behavior.[25] This fascination with the anti-social anti-hero not only reinforces people who identify with this ideology but it also feeds liberal fantasies.

Just as prestige TV caters to the elite by differentiating its product from the debased common culture of the masses, elite centrists alienate the working class by advertising the superiority of their knowledge and cultural habits. This sense that the liberal elites look down at the uncultured masses has helped to push the working class into the hands of the Right even when the policies of the Right do not help them.[26] There is thus a real political effect of the cultural divide generated by the discourse surrounding prestige TV. In creating a strict opposition between the elites and the masses, the promotion of prestige TV only intensifies the sense of upper-middle class liberal snobbery.

Defending Liberal Democracy

To explain the foundations of contemporary centrist ideology, we have to return to the roots of the modern notion of liberalism. As a product of the European Enlightenment, democratic law and subjectivity are based on the necessary but impossible ideals of neutrality, equality, and objectivity.[27] According to modern liberal beliefs, everyone is supposed to be treated equally by the law as one examines evidence from an impartial perspective. Even though this ideology has

6 Introduction

a bias against bias, it still promotes particular ideas and beliefs; however, the main objective is to promote social and legal equality centered on the use of impersonal, universal laws and rights.[28] Liberal democracy, then, is not about compromise or the privileging of individual freedom over social control—this modern ideology relies on avoiding the pitfalls of both tyranny and anarchy through the adoption of shared rules and a legal system employing the neutral judgment of empirical evidence.[29]

Through their relentless focus on the truth, both modern science and law ideally require a clear and transparent representation of facts, and therefore personal beliefs and feelings do not play a role. One reason why I am stressing this definition of modernity is that it is vital to see how contemporary "liberals" have moved away from these guiding principles. Instead of being the representatives of science and democracy, many centrists are driven by a repressed pursuit of profit, privilege, and power.[30] This capitalist compulsion that reveals itself in careerism and the selling out of the working class is often hidden by virtue-signaling and a superficial commitment to Left-wing beliefs.[31]

My understanding of centrist ideology is largely drawn from my experience working in higher education. Although many still see universities as "liberal" institutions, the truth is that they often rely on generating and maintaining economic inequality.[32] Not only do the selective admission standards of elite schools enhance the power of the wealthy and place the unwealthy in debt, but the tenured professors rely on exploiting the labor of adjuncts and graduate students.[33] While the majority of the faculty are now denied basic rights and a living wage, the elite professors and administrators hide their greed and power behind calls for diversity and equal opportunity.[34] This virtue signaling allows competitive capitalists the ability to repress their own complicity as they tend to blame the state for the ills of their institution.

My understanding of centrist ideology and subjectivity is in part derived from Robert Nisbet's *The Degradation of the Academic Dogma*.[35] Nisbet's argument is that the undermining of the liberal public mission of universities started after World War II when federal funds poured into these institutions to conduct Cold War research. When the faculty in the sciences realized that they could increase their prestige and earnings by dedicating themselves to government-funded research, they were incentivized to devalue teaching and shared governance. In order to maintain the façade that instruction was still the core mission of these schools, responsibility for teaching shifted to untenured faculty and graduate students. What Nisbet's narrative then teaches us is that liberal institutions were not destroyed by outside forces; instead, individuals acting on capitalistic incentives chose anti-social greed over the public good. In turn, this emphasis on prestigious careers was later hidden by the performance of progressive values, which did nothing to challenge the internal hierarchies and destructive social effects of this transformed liberal institution.

The invention of prestige TV should therefore be read in relation to the undermining of modern liberal institutions and the contradictory ideology of centrists who tend to produce and consume this mode of media.[36] On a fundamental level, the professional upper-middle class is divided between anti-social careerism and a desire to be seen as having good intentions by conforming to progressive values.

Method

Instead of framing my analysis by a conservative, Leftist, Right-wing, or centrist view, I seek to apply universal concepts derived from the theory and practice of psychoanalysis.[37] Part of this process entails not using the reductive frames of liberal vs. conservative or Right vs. Left. Since liberal democracy and science rely on employing shared concepts and methods in a neutral and unbiased way, one of the goals of this book is to reveal how cultural material can be examined in a scientific manner. Of course, many people see psychoanalysis as unscientific, and so it will be necessary to show how Freud's fundamental concepts are based on empirical truth.

Since Freud insists that both the artist and the audience are not aware of the primary processes shaping unconscious material, it is essential to reveal both the content and form of cultural fantasies.[38] In fact, because we are driven to avoid tension and conflict, we seek to repress anti-social impulses that make us feel shame and guilt. When these feelings are repressed or denied, they return through the process of projecting our own rejected thoughts and emotions onto devalued others.[39] Thus, in order to make unconscious fantasies conscious, the focus on escape and pleasure has to be reversed.

Psychoanalysis also pushes us to ask how does the television actually affect its audience? According to this psychoanalytic approach, it is not just mirroring or identification that defines the relation between television and its audience; rather, there are often conflicting unconscious mental processes that are triggered. Much of what TV does is to reinforce pre-existing frames and associations, but it can also create new unconscious connections as it caters to particular modes of pathology. In a society saturated by media representations, all aspects of life, including politics, become influenced and shaped by cultural fantasies. Moreover, political affiliations are themselves affected by specific psychopathologies as a feedback loop is set up between the individual and culture.[40] Therefore, if we want to understand politics today, we need to comprehend how culture influences individuals and how individuals shape the media.

My approach is against the notion that television systematically indoctrinates its audience into a particular ideology; however, I also want to insist that ideologies are reinforced and shaped by media productions.[41] I desire to avoid the pluralistic, centrist approach that claims television is just an open market of ideas with no strong effect on the audience. This model of pluralism is a product of the centrist ideology of ironic conformity: Void of any real values, including the values of liberal democracy, the centrists seek to cater to a mass audience by circulating contradictory and conflicting ideological representations. While I do offer a criticism of contemporary prestige TV, I am not lamenting the loss of conservative traditional values.

8 Introduction

One important point I want to make from the start is that it does not matter if a program critiques capitalism or racism if the criticism is viewed through the lens of ironic distance.[42] Furthermore, television does not have only one purpose since the goal of making more money is challenged by the desire of artists to display their creativity, knowledge, and wit. Therefore, even if we can follow the academic Marxist insistence that TV is driven by the profit motive and the legitimation of modern capitalist ideology, the power of the audience to understand and misunderstand what is being presented means that a deterministic model cannot be applied.[43] On the other hand, we do not want to argue that people are totally free to use television for their own purposes; we have to insist on a dialectical relation between culture and the individual.

The Psychoanalytic Interpretation of Prestige TV

The main series that this book examines are *The Sopranos, Breaking Bad, The Wire, House of Cards, Dexter, Game of Thrones*, and *Succession*. All of these programs have been associated with prestige TV, but it is often unclear what connects these shows other than their tremendous popularity and critical acclaim.[44] On the most basic level, what they have in common is a sense of gritty realism through their mostly uncensored presentation of sex, violence, and profanity.[45] These productions also highlight complex characters who are morally ambiguous and often act in extreme ways.[46] Moreover, since these shows often do not include commercial breaks and they do not have to cater to a mass audience, they allow for longer, sustained plots and audience immersion, which often results in complex, multi-level storytelling.[47] Ultimately, the enhanced attention to detail enables these prestige programs to create a strong combination of realism and fiction.

Book Outline

In Chapter 2, I examine *The Sopranos* in order to reveal the repressed centrist attraction to Right-wing ideology and subjectivity. Since Tony Soprano shares many important characteristics with Donald Trump, we can understand the "liberal" media's obsession with Trump and other libertarian politicians through our analysis of how the audience relates to the depiction of a fictional mob boss.[48] On one level, Tony presents the libertarian backlash against women, minorities, political correctness, and the Leftist super-ego, but on another level, his therapy and self-awareness place his anti-social libertarian pathology within a centrist ironic discourse.[49] Not only do his actions enable the audience to live through his transgressive behavior in a shared cultural fantasy, but Tony's capitalist compulsion reinforces the "liberal" audience's own disavowed commitment to capitalist survivalism. One reason, then, why centrist liberals have been so bad at defeating someone like Trump is that they have themselves produced and supported libertarian cultural fantasies. Furthermore, while Tony laments the loss of traditional values and social hierarchies, what this show also depicts is the radical misunderstanding of liberal democracy by the "liberal" media.[50]

In Chapter 3, this analysis of the centrist relation to Right-wing ideology and Neoliberal capitalism is applied to *Breaking Bad*.[51] While the main character, Walter White, at first argues that his turn to crime is driven by his desire to help his family survive, we learn at the end that his transgressions were motivated by the way they made him feel powerful and important. In the structure of this story, it turns out that capitalism is the only solution to the problems caused by capitalism as Walter's criminality is driven by a need to make more money at all costs. With this form of capitalist realism, we find the centrist commitment to careerism as a source of individual survival and enjoyment.[52] Since no alternative to the current system is seen as possible, all one can do is further commit to a system one condemns. From this perspective, the audience is not simply identifying with Walter's compulsive capitalism—the audience is also critiquing and morally condemning his actions. It is, therefore, necessary to take a doubled perspective on both the content and the audience's relation to this production.

Chapter 4 looks at *The Wire* as a paradigmatic example of centrist ideology and subjectivity. Through its gritty documentation of urban violence, criminality, and drug use, the series originally allowed a mostly white-upper-middle-class audience access to a threatening world at a safe distance.[53] In a mode of virtual slumming, centrists project their own repressed sexual and violent impulses onto a dark other so that the TV audience can gain access to their anti-social impulses from the safe comfort of their homes.[54] This mode of "liberal" media reveals how centrists help to re-circulate conservative racist and sexist stereotypes and prejudices while still maintaining a sense of being morally pure and righteous.

In Chapter 5, I turn to *House of Cards* to see how centrist ideology results in an ironic and cynical approach to liberal democracy.[55] Through its depictions of the ruthless pragmatism of Frank Underwood, we gain insight into how liberalism has been undermined by a focus on individual careers and self-promotion. The centrist careerism shaping this series is coupled with the use of direct addresses to the audience, which creates a doubled, ironic discourse. At the same moment we are asked to recognize the evil intentions of Underwood, we are also made complicit when he shares hidden information with us.

In Chapter 6, the Showtime series *Dexter* is analyzed by looking at how the audience is made to feel guilty pleasure through an ambivalent depiction of a serial killer.[56] Since the main character is only supposed to kill people who the legal system fails to prosecute, we see how the underlying fantasy is driven by a lost faith in our modern liberal democratic institutions. Vigilante justice is therefore presented as a just response to a failed social order, which remains the only game in town.[57] Furthermore, through the use of Dexter's narrative voice-over, the audience is made complicit as a doubled, ironic representation is produced.

In Chapter 7, *Game of Thrones* is read as depicting the unconscious backlash against the fight for female equality.[58] Although some believe that this popular

10 Introduction

series presents how powerful women gain power by the end, what really happens is that the revolt of the female is pathologized and contained through an ironic depiction of gender conflict. Moreover, by playing out current culture wars through the depiction of a fictional Medieval period, the show is able to both say and unsay the same thing in a doubled, self-reflexive discourse. A key to this interpretation will be the revelation of a hidden centrist fear of the maternal super-ego.[59]

In Chapter 8, I conclude by presenting *Succession* as another centrist fantasy concerning the libertarian Right. Based partially on a fictional representation of Rupert Murdoch and Fox News, this series combines the serious with the unserious as it updates *King Lear* for contemporary culture. With the possible death of the powerful father, the show concerns not only who and what will replace the old dying order but why a seemingly liberal audience would want to identity with the libertarian Right.

In my analysis of these different programs, I focus on deepening our understanding of the psychopathology of obsessional narcissism, which helps to shape the values and psychology of upper-middle class professionals and political centrists. Of course, the main readers of this book will be the group I am critiquing, but my hope is that this work can provide conceptual tools to make our unconscious processes conscious.

Notes

1 Newman, Michael Z. "Quality TV as liberal TV." *Western Humanities Review* 70.3 (2016): 70–79.
2 Samuels, Robert. *Educating inequality: beyond the political myths of higher education and the job market*. Routledge, 2017.
3 Bourdieu, Pierre. *Distinction: a social critique of the judgement of taste*. Routledge, 2019. 499–525.
4 Lobato, Ramon. "Streaming services and the changing global geography of television." *Handbook on Geographies of Technology*. Edward Elgar Publishing, 2017.
5 Newman, Michael Z., and Elana Levine. *Legitimating television: media convergence and cultural status*. Routledge, 2012.
6 Newman, Michael Z., and Elana Levine. *Legitimating television: media convergence and cultural status*. Routledge, 2012.
7 Hedges, Chris. *Death of the liberal class*. Vintage Books Canada, 2011.
8 Pickard, Victor. "Media failures in the age of Trump." *The Political Economy of Communication* 4.2 (2017): 118–122.
9 Samuels, Robert. "(Liberal) Narcissism." *Routledge handbook of psychoanalytic political theory*. Routledge, 2019. 151–161.
10 Hutcheon, Linda. "Beginning to theorize postmodernism." *Textual Practice* 1.1 (1987): 10–31.
11 Gartman, David. "Culture as class symbolization or mass reification? A critique of Bourdieu's distinction." *American Journal of Sociology* 97.2 (1991): 421–447.
12 Freud, Sigmund. "Predisposition to the obsessional neurosis." *The Psychoanalytic Review (1913–1957)* 21 (1934): 347.
13 Stewart, Matthew. *The 9.9 percent: the new aristocracy that is entrenching inequality and warping our culture*. New York: Simon & Schuster, 2021.
14 Fisher, Mark. *Capitalist realism: is there no alternative?* John Hunt Publishing, 2009.

15 Lasch, Christopher. *The culture of narcissism: American life in an age of diminishing expectations.* W. W. Norton & Company, 2018.

16 Arzheimer, Kai. *Working-class parties 2.0? Competition between centre left and extreme right parties.* Routledge, 2013.

17 Rivera, Lauren A. *Pedigree.* Princeton University Press, 2016.

18 Samuels, Robert. "Beyond Hillary Clinton: obsessional narcissism and the failure of the liberal class." *Psychoanalyzing the Left and Right after Donald Trump.* Palgrave Macmillan, Cham, 2016. 31–59.

19 Holladay, Holly Willson, and Melissa A. Click. "Hating Skyler White." *Anti-Fandom: Dislike and Hate in the Digital Age* 24 (2019): 147.

20 Vincent, Christopher J. *Paying respect to The Sopranos: a psychosocial analysis.* McFarland, 2014.

21 Genz, Stéphanie. "'I'm not going to fight them, I'm going to fuck them': sexist liberalism and gender (A) politics in Game of Thrones." *Women of ice and fire: gender, Game of Thrones and multiple media engagements.* 2016. 243–266.

22 Samuels, Robert. "Simon Clarke and the politics and psychoanalysis of racism." *Psychoanalysis, Culture & Society* 25.1 (2020): 96–100.

23 Ruiz, Maria Isabel Romero. "Neo-Victorian families: gender, sexual and cultural politics." *Miscelánea: A Journal of English and American Studies* 46 (2012).

24 Lukes, Steven. "The meanings of 'individualism'." *Journal of the History of Ideas* 32.1 (1971): 45–66.

25 Bodell, Harry. "From Tony Soprano to Donald Trump: situating the rhetoric of the 2016 Trump presidential campaign in the antihero genre." Graduate Research Theses & Dissertations (2019): 3208. https://huskiecommons.lib.niu.edu/allgraduate-thesesdissertations/3208.

26 Isenberg, Nancy, and Andrew Burstein. "Cosmopolitanism vs. provincialism: how the politics of place hurts America." *The Hedgehog Review* 19.2 (2017): 58–70.

27 Rauch, Jonathan. *The constitution of knowledge: a defense of truth.* Brookings Institution Press, 2021.

28 Pagden, Anthony. *The enlightenment: and why it still matters.* Oxford University Press, 2013.

29 McMurran, Mary Helen. "The new cosmopolitanism and the eighteenth century." *Eighteenth-Century Studies* (2013): 19–38.

30 Hedges, Chris. *Death of the liberal class.* Vintage Books, Canada, 2011.

31 Saltman, Kenneth J. "'Privilege-checking,' 'virtue-signaling,' and 'safe spaces': what happens when cultural politics is privatized and the body replaces argument." *symplokē* 26.1–2 (2017): 403–409.

32 Samuels, Robert. *Educating inequality: beyond the political myths of higher education and the job market.* Routledge, 2017.

33 Bousquet, Marc, and Cary Nelson. *How the university works.* New York University Press, 2008.

34 Murray, Darrin S. "The precarious new faculty majority: communication and instruction research and contingent labor in higher education." *Communication Education* 68.2 (2019): 235–245.

35 Nisbet, Robert A. *The degradation of the academic dogma.* Routledge, 2018.

36 Newman, Michael Z., and Elana Levine. *Legitimating television: media convergence and cultural status.* Routledge, 2012.

37 Samuels, Robert. "Logos, global justice, and the reality principle." *Zizek and the rhetorical unconscious.* Palgrave Macmillan, Cham, 2020. 65–86.

38 Freud, Sigmund. *Jokes and their relation to the unconscious.* W. W. Norton & Company, 1960.

39 Samuels, Robert. "Simon Clarke and the politics and psychoanalysis of racism." *Psychoanalysis, Culture & Society* 25.1 (2020): 96–100.

40 Samuels, Robert. *Generation X and the rise of the entertainment subject.* Rowman & Littlefield, 2021.

12 Introduction

41 Kellner, Douglas. *Television and the crisis of democracy.* Routledge, 2018.

42 Hutcheon, Linda. "The politics of postmodernism: parody and history." *Cultural Critique* 5 (1986): 179–207.

43 Jenkins, Henry. *Textual poachers: television fans and participatory culture.* Routledge, 2012.

44 Wittwer, Preston. "Say my name: Walter White as Rumpelstiltskin and reading 'Breaking Bad' as a classic fairy tale." *The Midwest Quarterly* 59.1 (2017): 70–81.

45 Sepinwall, Alan. *The revolution was televised: the cops, crooks, slingers, and slayers who changed TV drama forever.* Simon and Schuster, 2013.

46 Martin, Brett. *Difficult men: behind the scenes of a creative revolution: from The Sopranos and The Wire to Mad Men and Breaking Bad.* Penguin, 2013.

47 Santo, Avi. *Para-television and discourses of distinction: the culture of production at HBO.* Routledge, 2009.

48 Poniewozik, James. *Audience of one: Donald Trump, television, and the fracturing of America.* Liveright Publishing, 2019.

49 Samuels, Robert. "Catharsis: the politics of enjoyment." *Zizek and the rhetorical unconscious.* Palgrave Macmillan, Cham, 2020. 7–31.

50 Parenti, Michael. "The myth of a liberal media." *The Humanist* 55.1 (1995): 7.

51 Lee, David R. *What's the matter with Walter? The privatization of everything in Breaking Bad.* Harvard University, 2016.

52 Fisher, Mark. *Capitalist realism: is there no alternative?* John Hunt Publishing, 2009.

53 Johnson, Michael. "White authorship and the counterfeit politics of verisimilitude on The Wire." *African Americans on television: racing for ratings,* D. Leonard & L. Guerrero, Praeger, 2013.

54 Walters, Ben. "The Wire for tourists?" *Film Quarterly* 62.2 (2008): 64.

55 Shea, Brendan. "House of cards as philosophy: democracy on trial." *The Palgrave Handbook of Popular Culture as Philosophy. Palgrave,* 2020: 1–22.

56 Granelli, Steven, and Jason Zenor. "Decoding 'The Code': reception theory and moral judgment of Dexter." *International Journal of Communication* 10 (2016): 23.

57 Butler, Paul. "Retribution, for liberals." *UCLA Law Review* 46 (1998): 1873.

58 Ferreday, Debra. "Game of Thrones, rape culture and feminist fandom." *Australian Feminist Studies* 30.83 (2015): 21–36.

59 Spolander, Rebecca. "The fear of Mrs. Bates: the use of psychoanalytical aspects, anticipation and retrospection in Robert Bloch's Psycho." *DIVA* (2018): 31.

2

THE SOPRANOS

Make TV Elite Again

Why are "liberal" audiences fascinated by a violent criminal who laments the loss of traditional values and fears the rise of strong women?[1] Besides the attraction to repressed violent and sexual impulses, what explains the centrist investment in producing and watching anti-social behavior? Moreover, what is the political effect of the aesthetic representation of social deviance?[2] In short, how did a series like *The Sopranos* help to pave the way for Donald Trump to become president?[3]

Although Trump's rise to power can be derived from his promotion of conservative judges, tax cuts for the wealthy, and racist, nationalistic rhetoric, his ability to win a national election after the exposure of so many personal moral faults needs to be explained by an additional factor, which is the "liberal" media's attraction to anti-social personalities. Of course, mainstream channels, like CBS, said they gave Trump so much free coverage because that is what people wanted to watch; however, the question is why did a mostly Democrat-identified audience desire to constantly be informed about this Republican candidate?[4] Was this just a case of people trying to keep their eye on a dangerous enemy? Or was the liberal audience enjoying the depiction of exactly what they claimed to hate? While *The Sopranos* was made years before Trump's rise to power, the show helps to trace the centrist investment in what it claims to hate. After all, Trump is just a symptom of a sociopathic mode of capitalism and pleasure-seeking that has been gaining power in the United States and other countries since the advent of the modern welfare state. As the personification of libertarian Neoliberalism, Trump's psychopathology can be related to a culture of borderline personality disorder dominated by impulsive selfishness and anti-social exploitation often fueled by a masculine libido. However, what my analysis seeks to uncover is the secret complicity of "liberal" narcissism in perpetuating borderline personalities. As Freud posits that neurotics fantasize about what perverts perform, narcissists produce cultural fantasies centered on borderline acts.

DOI: 10.4324/9781003352600-2

14 *The Sopranos*

Psychoanalyzing Cultural Fantasies

From a psychoanalytic perspective, cultural fantasies allow people the opportunity to experience repressed desires in a disguised and excusable way.[5] Moreover, according to Freud, both the producer and the receiver of art remain unconscious as repressed material is able to circulate without anyone really knowing what is happening.[6] One of the main reasons for this lack of conscious awareness is that people seek to hide from themselves their own immoral and unwanted impulses.[7] The other major cause for this lack of knowing is that automatic symbolic processes function without our intention or control.[8] Furthermore, humans are driven to pursue pleasure, but as Freud insists, pleasure is based on a release of both mental and physical tension, which means that we seek to escape reality and conscious reflection.[9]

According to Freud's theory of humor, the producer of a joke gives the audience pleasure with the tacit agreement that the audience will not hold the producer responsible for what is presented.[10] We can think of this theory as the basic psychoanalytic model of popular culture: the audience is given enjoyment in exchange for giving up critical judgment. The pursuit of happiness, then, leads to a suspension of critical analysis.[11] What we then find in a society increasingly dominated by the culture industry is this focus on enjoyment and escape in all aspects of life.[12]

The next question concerns how does mass media affect the audience if the major result of popular culture is to provide pleasure at the cost of criticism? Furthermore, if these representations are circulated on a purely unconscious level, how do they shape actual behavior? For example, if I secretly identify with Tony Soprano's violent outbursts, in what ways are my beliefs and values being affected? Does his liberation from the oppressive maternal super-ego motivate me to also seek to escape a feminized version of the social censor? Or does the circulation of unconscious fears and desires simply reinforce what I already think and believe?

My hypothesis is that the repetition of certain cultural fantasies not only changes what is tolerated in a particular society but also provides highly influential frames for interpreting the self and the world on an unconscious and unintentional level.[13] Moreover, political ideologies and affiliations are not primarily based on policies and public issues; instead, specific political ideologies cater to particular psychopathologies, which are shaped by shared cultural fantasies.[14] For example, the libertarian Right-wing backlash against feminism, political correctness, and identity politics caters to an impulsive, masculine, anti-social borderline personality reinforced by the cultural fantasy of the maternal super-ego threatening to castrate the phallic male.[15] We see this fantasy frame play out in *The Sopranos* as Tony's anxiety and violence is represented as a result of his toxic mother and the loss of traditional male authority.[16]

A Story of Decline and Threat

A close reading of the pilot episode reveals that the show's creator, David Chase, obsesses over the notion that standards, traditions, and values have been eroded to such an extent that men no longer know how they should act and behave.[17] This narrative of cultural decline is coupled with the presence of women who constantly nag, threaten, and humiliate the central male character.[18] Not only has Tony been forced to see a female therapist to talk about his feelings, but he is pushed to medicate his anxiety. In response, Tony asks what happened to the strong silent type, like Gary Cooper, as he fears that not only will talking about his feelings emasculate him, but it will also make him vulnerable to other men.[19] As he sees the young male members of his group fail to respect tradition and hierarchy, he refuses to understand that what is really destroying the old order of patriarchy is not the rise of female power but the unrestrained pursuit of pleasure and profit.

As Marx insisted, modern capitalism melts away all solid, premodern traditions, borders, and beliefs as exchange value replaces moral and ethical values.[20] However, instead of confronting the destructive aspects of compulsive, nihilistic capitalism, the show feeds the unconscious cultural fantasy of blaming women for undermining masculine identity.[21] Thus, if Tony's panic is triggered by his fears that he cannot keep his family together, this anxiety is caused in part by a denial of the ways the pure pursuit of enjoyment and profit ends in self-destruction.[22] Tony is not only an anti-social addict who cannot control his impulses and emotions, but he is also a white male who believes that he is losing his identity due to the growing power of women, minorities, and the young.[23] Since he does not want to give up his addictions, he has to blame his problems on devalued others. However, the question remains of why does a centrist liberal audience want to see this drama unfold and why was it created by a "liberal" media culture?[24]

We usually think of the angry white male supporter of Trump and other Right-wing politicians as the product of either the manipulation of powerful capitalists or the victims of economic degradation.[25] However, Tony Soprano represents the angry white male who is driven by his desire to enjoy without any restraint. As a fantasy of the centrist imagination, he reflects the repressed sexual and violent impulses that have been sacrificed for the goal of social stability. In the split consciousness of this narcissistic mode of psychopathology, the desire to be seen as good and competent requires the repression of feelings that are considered to be anti-social.[26] When these repressed desires return in the form of cultural fantasies, they not only normalize deviant behavior but they also provide an effective mode of denial.

Just as the Right needs the Left so that it can unify its supporters behind a shared enemy, liberal centrists often seek to appease the politically correct Left through virtue signaling as they also produce and consume fantasies of the libertine, libertarian Right.[27] Meanwhile, the Left defines itself against the Right and conservatives as it attacks centrist liberals for not being woke enough.[28] In this polarizing structure, each group produces solidarity by defining itself against

16 *The Sopranos*

the other group, which causes heightened extremism and polarization.[29] For traditional conservatives, the main goal is to conserve social order by reinforcing a hierarchy through the repetition and policing of stereotypes, prejudices, and traditional identity markers.[30] Yet, contemporary conservatives have learned that if they want to maintain power, they have to form a coalition with amoral capitalists who share a hatred of the Left and liberals.[31] Unintentionally, centrist popular culture feeds this Republican coalition by circulating racist and sexist fantasies from a position of denial.[32] Moreover, through its resistance to directly critique capitalism and labor issues, the professional liberal class gives a free pass to economic nihilism.[33]

The Fall of the Democrats

One of the great current issues of political debate is what has caused the move of working-class voters in the United States from the Democratic Party to the Republican Party.[34] We know that a key aspect of this transition has been the loss of unionized jobs in manufacturing. Since, in the past, these protected workers, often without college degrees, belonged to powerful organizations that made large political contributions to the Democratic Party, it made sense for the Democrats and organized labor to work together; however, once factories started to be outsourced and automated, many white workers no longer had a reason to support Democrats.[35] This transformation was largely driven, then, by an economic drive to increase profits in a globalized labor and consumer market.[36]

At the same time that unionized jobs were being reduced by the millions, the Democratic Party realized that it could replace the funds of organized labor with suburban professionals.[37] However, the Democrats still wanted to be seen as the party of workers, and this created a conflicted, hypocritical mindset. Furthermore, as higher education became a key component of economic and social mobility, the Democratic Party started to see education as the great equalizer, even though it functioned overall to increase inequality and decrease social mobility.[38] The Democratic Party, thus, became an organization that mouthed progressive rhetoric as it pursued a mostly Republican agenda, and it is this dynamic that often shapes the ideology and psychopathology of the original consumers and producers of prestige TV.

In response to the Democratic Party's reduced commitment to workers without college degrees, the Republican Party has been able to attract these voters by offering them a culture war instead of an economic solution.[39] By turning its attention to identity politics, political correctness, and the welfare state, Republicans unify conservatives and Right-wing libertarians through a shared hatred of the Left.[40] A key aspect of this coalition is to create a polarized perspective with clear differences on a mostly cultural level. In turn, the Left has fed this dynamic by shifting its focus from labor and capitalism to issues concerning race, gender, and sexual orientation.[41] With this move from class war to culture war, we can begin to understand the centrist investment in a show like *The Sopranos*.

The Decline of the White Male

Throughout the pilot episode of this show, Tony Soprano obsessively returns to a sense of cultural decline and a loss of masculine identity.[42] Not only does he wonder if the sun is setting on the empire, but he ties his first panic attack to a sense that he was born too late to fully enjoy his mob life. As he tells his psychiatrist, Dr. Melfi, "That morning of the day I got sick? I'd been thinking: it's good to be in a thing from the ground floor. I came too late for that, I know. But lately, I'm getting the feeling I might be in at the end. That the best is over." Similar to Trump's call to Make America Great Again, Tony laments the loss of an older cultural period that was shaped by a sense of tradition, respect, and male dominance.[43] In fact, in response to his self-analysis, Dr. Melfi responds, "Many Americans, I think, feel this." As the potential voice of reason, the good doctor lends credence to Tony's sense of the passing of the conservative patriarchal order. While the cause of this loss could be ascribed to a changing economic system, Tony stresses a lack of traditional moral values: "Take my father. He never reached the heights like me. But in ways he had it better. He had his people — they had their standards. They had pride. Today what do we got?" For Tony, even if he makes more money than his father made, he wonders if his father had it better because the old order still had standards.[44]

In order to flesh out what he is complaining about, Tony uses the example of his nephew, Christopher, who is seen as epitomizing a lack of older standards. Tony tells Christopher that he should have called a man in the morning, but his nephew shows a lack of work ethic since he stayed out late and did not wake up in time. Christopher adds, "I was nauseous this morning. My mom told me I shouldn't even go in today." By introducing the mother into the conversation, we see how women will be represented as undermining both men and the old way of doing things.[45]

Tied to this sense of being part of a dying culture is Tony's complaint that kids today have become spoiled. In discussing his son A.J. with his uncle, Junior, Tony says, "Don't buy him anything big. We overindulge him." Here, we see how the loss of a strong work ethic and respect for tradition is blamed on the way parents today cater to their children. Instead of looking at how the shift to a consumerist mode of capitalism has transformed all past social structures, the show tends to blame discrete individuals for their lack of moral standards.[46] Of course, the irony of this story is that the person telling other people to act in a more respectful and moral way is a sociopathic criminal who transgresses every ethical and legal standard for his own personal pleasure and gain.

However, what does give this show a more complex and ironic structure is that Tony is forced to externalize his feelings and understandings.[47] The series,

18 *The Sopranos*

then, does not simply present his borderline impulses and actions, and the primary reason for this complication is the use of psychoanalysis both inside and outside of the consulting room.[48] For example, due to his ambivalence concerning his need to talk about his feelings and life, Tony laments about the good old days when men were strong and silent. As he tells Dr. Melfi, "Whatever happened to Gary Cooper? The strong silent type. That was an American. He wasn't in touch with his feelings. He just did what he had to do!" It is interesting that Tony here identifies the strong silent male with the America of the past.[49] Just as Trump wants to make American great again by returning to some unknown mythologized past, Tony feels that his talking to a shrink prevents him from recapturing an older, idealized model of masculinity: "Unfortunately, what they didn't know was once they got Gary Cooper in touch with his feelings, they wouldn't be able to shut him up! Dysfunction this! Dysfunction that!" Here, therapy is seen as undermining masculinity through a form of feminization.[50]

In fact, Tony's sense that American has been undermined by the rise of women in all aspects of society relates to his belief that his mother destroyed his father, and she also desires to destroy him: "Now that my father's dead? He's a saint. When he was alive? … My dad was tough. Ran his own crew. Guy like that and my mother wore him down to a little nub. He was a squeaking gerbil–when he died." We see here how Tony and the show itself tend to put the blame for the loss of a former model of masculinity on women in general and mothers in particular.[51] We, therefore, witness an underlying sexism that pervades the program and connects with a repressed sense that it is women who are really at fault. Furthermore, it is my argument that this blaming of mothers and females is in part due to the way that destructive aspects of compulsive capitalism are displaced onto women in the form of an unconscious cultural fantasy. Since Tony and the centrist mindset do not want to condemn their own investment in an addictive mode of capitalist competition and consumption, they produce narratives where females are blamed for the breakdown of the nuclear family and the loss of masculine identity.

Tony's sense of being emasculated comes to the foreground in a dream that he recounts to Dr. Melfi:

> I had a dream last night. My belly button was a philips-head screw. And I was working unscrewing it. And when I got it all the way unscrewed my … my penis fell off. And I'm running around with it yelling, trying to find this mechanic used to work on my Lincoln when I drove Lincolns and he was supposed to screw it back on, only this bird swooped down and took it in its beak and flew off with it and I woke up.

Within this dream of castration, Tony reveals his deep fear that he is losing his sense of being a man by talking about his feelings and by the way his mother keeps attacking him and bringing him down.[52] Similar to Freud's reading of Leonardo da Vinci's paintings, the birds can be equated with the castration caused by the attacking maternal super-ego.[53]

Of course, there is much more to *The Sopranos* than an underlying sexist fear of female-led destruction, but what is often missed is the way this unconscious cultural fantasy serves to shape both the libertarian Right-wing backlash and the repressed centrist defense of unbridled capitalism. One of the key things that this series and other prestige TV programs accomplish is the translation of class conflict into a culture war.[54] From this perspective, the problem, then, is not that jobs are being automated and outsourced, the real issue is that women and other minority groups are undermining men and masculinity. Furthermore, the real victims in this cultural fantasy are the powerful, wealthy men who are constantly being attacked by a feminized super-ego.[55] By turning the powerful into victims and moving our attention from class to gender and race, these "liberal" productions feed a Right-wing rebellion against liberalism itself.

A Brief History of Liberalism

To understand the cultural moment of prestige TV, it is important to comprehend how modern liberalism was developed and how it has been undermined. On the most basic level, modern liberalism is shaped by creating an alternative to premodern religion, feudalism, and monarchy.[56] While the conservative premodern culture seeks to conserve the social hierarchy, modern society replaces religion with science, feudalism with capitalism, and monarchy with democracy.[57] Instead of basing identity, value, and truth on an inherited and predetermined social order, modernity seeks to discover truth through the scientific method, which relies on the empirical testing of evidence from a neutral perspective.[58] Likewise, liberal democracy relies on the ideal of equality, which aims to replace the authority of the ruler with the universal rights of the ruled. Moreover, while the older feudal system was based on a fixed social and class hierarchy, modern capitalism allows for geographical and economic mobility.[59]

From a postmodern Leftist perspective, the modern goals of equality and social mobility are betrayed by the exclusion of minority groups, and yet, the goal of most progressive social movements is to expand democratic rights to all people.[60] In response to this revolution from below, the Right seeks to reverse postmodern politics and culture by returning to premodern traditional values.[61] However, this counter-revolution relies on forming a coalition between conservative religious fundamentalists and free market libertarians. The trick, then, is how you unite two groups with opposite values since the conservatives want to dictate social behavior, while the libertarians want to focus on the liberated individual who is free to act as he or she wants.[62] One of the main ways this combination of opposites is achieved is by uniting around a shared hatred of the common enemy—the Left. Since both sides do not want to be controlled by minority-based identity politics or political correctness, there is a common interest in targeting an oppressive Left-wing discourse.

How the Wealthy Bond with the Poor

However, this reactionary ideology also has to find a way of promoting the interests of the wealthy as it caters to the desires of the white working poor.[63] For instance, after the Great Recession of 2008, the people who caused and profited from destructive financial speculation were somehow able to rally the working poor against the government and not the financial elites.[64] At the same time that the wealthiest institutions and people were bailed out and protected, Republicans found a way to get white working-class people to support a supposed billionaire for president. Part of this process was to show how the Democrats failed in producing policies to protect the white working poor, but much of the magic came from the ability to represent the wealthiest and most powerful men as being victims worthy of sympathy and support.[65]

Not only did the rich demand tax cuts and de-regulation, but they also wanted to be seen as the victims of society. By representing themselves as the losers of a culture war, the real class war was hidden and reversed.[66] Just as Tony Soprano represents himself as being the victim of his mother, his wife, and the feminization of culture, other sociopathic capitalists are able to present themselves as the true victims of political correctness and identity politics.[67] Moreover, in order to bond with the working poor, it was necessary to present Republican politicians as real and authentic in contrast to the hypocrisy of Democrats.[68] Trump was able to play on this produced authenticity by refusing to be scripted or politically correct.[69]

What is so fascinating is at the same time the Right was pretending to be authentic and real, prestige TV was gaining attention by presenting relatively uncensored sex, violence, and profanity.[70] Thus, if network television appeared to be fake, censored, and scripted, cable TV was allowed to transgress these restrictions.[71] The aesthetics of these new series, therefore, matched the aesthetics of the political Right, and yet the myth of the "liberal" media was maintained. In fact, we know that many of the creators and writers of these shows consider themselves to be liberal Democrats, and so we have to ask how does their affiliation with the Democratic party relate to their production of a libertarian culture?[72]

One answer to this question can be ascribed to the way that obsessional narcissists repress their sexual and violent impulses and then transform those drives into fantasies.[73] Since they want to maintain a self-image of being good and pure, they have to deny their own anti-social impulses. Popular culture then becomes a safe space for releasing pent-up, repressed feelings. Thus, we may like to watch a sociopathic criminal because we can experience our own repressed desires through his actions.[74] Furthermore, since we can always tell ourselves that we are only watching a show of a fictional character, we do not have to take our own investments in the character seriously. Also, when we react negatively to the transgressions of the criminal, we can re-assure ourselves that we are good and moral. From this perspective, we enjoy libertarian fantasies because they give us a safe access to our own anti-social desires and impulses.

The question remains, though, of what effect this enjoyment of Right-wing fantasies has on our social and political order? Does the centrist production and consumption of anti-social behavior normalize deviance in an unconscious and unintentional way? For example, when we learn to feel sympathy for Tony Soprano, are we being trained to tolerate and accept a libertarian, libertine ideology? Even if we find this type of personality and behavior to be repulsive, isn't a key aspect of obsessional narcissism the combination of attraction and repulsion? For instance, when Leslie Moonves of CBS said that giving Trump so much coverage may not have been good for the country, but it was good for his company, he was not only admitting that journalism and democracy had been undermined by the profit-motive; he was also arguing that his centrist audience wanted to see more of this transgressive character.[75]

Perhaps centrist liberals wanted to watch Trump because they were so horrified by his speech and actions, but the analysis of prestige TV that I am presenting tells us something else. After all, we do not watch Tony Soprano because we want to keep an eye on him or rage against his anti-social activities: We watch because we are fascinated by the realization of our own repressed desires and impulses. It simply gives us enjoyment to view someone who can do and say what he feels. We also like the fact that we do not have to own our own anti-social passions because we can always tell ourselves that it is just a show.

Producing and Consuming Prestige

The centrist attraction to *The Sopranos* can also be related to the way that the once-debased mode of television consumption has been replaced by a system that differentiates between TV for the masses and prestige TV for the elites. According to Martin Z. Newman's and Elana Levine's *Legitimating Television,* critics and producers have used the idealization of specific cable shows to devalue mass television consumption, while prestige shows are celebrated for their connection to the high cultural realms of cinema and literature.[76] Therefore, even though Tony Soprano himself presents a working-class attitude, he is not only placed within an upper-middle-class neighborhood, but the show itself utilizes elite aesthetic formal elements. While HBO sought to promote the show as high art, it made sure to say that it was not like the regular television programs for the masses; this tough demanding series was presented as being more complex and artistic than the regular viewing fare.[77]

The production and promotion of prestige TV, then, fits well with the upper-middle-class mentality of centrist liberals who seek to have the best of everything.[78] As winners of the meritocracy, the professional class takes advantage of economic and social inequality by using their resources to outcompete the lower classes as the middle class continues to disappear.[79] For instance, we watch in the first season as Carmela uses her wealth and power to help get her daughter, Meadow, into a prestigious college.[80] Meanwhile, Tony socializes with wealthy professionals at their country club while his wife keeps on pushing him to move into even more expensive homes.[81]

22 *The Sopranos*

As Mathew Stewart writes in *The 9.9%*, the key to understanding the ideology of the upper-middle class is to realize how they have taken advantage of an unequal society by enhancing their wealth and power through the control of housing, college admissions, and cultural systems: "Money is never just about the money. Human beings always convert cold cash into good matches, elevated social status, higher education, better health, and political power—and then they turn around and exchange those other forms of advantage for money" (13).[82] Tony Soprano embodies this ideology by using the money generated from his criminal activities to gain access to the social institutions shaping the top 9.9%.[83] From this perspective, Tony presents the values and behaviors of centrist ideology, and yet due to his extreme behavior, the audience is able to disconnect from what they are seeing. The show then further mystifies the social order because it produces a combination of identification and denial.

According to Stewart, the ideology of the centrist 9.9% brings together seemingly good intentions with negative social effects:

> I take for granted that people will do whatever possible to secure a happy future for themselves, and there would in any case be no point in shaming them for doing what only comes naturally. I doubt that anybody sets off in the morning with the malicious intent of breaking up other people's families, perverting the system of education, shortening average life expectancy, raising average commute times to toxic levels, or profiting from the race hatred of other people. The point is just that that is what happens in the twilight of the meritocracy. Rising inequality takes good values and quietly twists them into bad ones. The unconscious hoarding that has come to define the life of the 9.9 percent is a response to this underlying condition, not the cause, and it is a response born of weakness, not strength. (14)

By taking advantage of corrupted liberal institutions in an unequal society, the people with the most wealth are able to reverse the invisible hand. In other words, against Adam Smith's libertarian notion that people acting selfishly will contribute unintentionally to the common good, we see the tragedy of the commons and the undermining of social trust in modern liberal democratic systems.[84]

When people just look out for themselves, their greed and anti-social behavior corrode the social contract and enable the rise of a criminal class. Once again, *The Sopranos* both reflects and blocks our understanding of this system, and this may be one reason why it is seen as a key product of prestige TV. In an ambivalent way, we turn to the media to see our own values and actions represented, but we also want to deny the negative social and personal effects of our investments. For Stewart, the culture and ideology of the upper-middle class rely on both reflected awareness and ignorance:

> The distinguishing feature of the 9.9 percent is not that it has advantages and is willing to use them, but that it confuses its privileges with artifacts

of nature. It sees its own virtues brightly in the mirror, and it has no trouble spotting the vices of other people. But it remains blind to the conditions on which both depend. That willful ignorance is the glue that holds the system together. It is our collective contribution to the triumph of the 0.1 percent and the fall of the 90 percent. Rising inequality makes accomplices of us all. (15)

Since we do not want to believe that we are contributing to inequality and poverty, we have to repress our awareness of what actually shapes our economic and political systems.[85] Prestige TV helps to enable this ideological mystification by coupling awareness with aesthetic distance. After all, we can always say that we are just watching a fiction and an extreme character, so the mirror at which we are staring can be considered not to matter.

White Privilege and the 9.9%

Within the context of *The Sopranos*, Carmela often embodies the upper-middle-class centrist who voices moral concerns as she profits from inequality and exploitation.[86] Although she tells Tony that he is going to hell for his criminal and adulterous behavior, she enjoys the lifestyle that is enabled by his anti-social activities. Moreover, she uses her husband's money and reputation to gain access to elite institutions, and so she reflects the ethos of the 9.9%. She also happens to be white, and as Stewart reminds us, since the 1970s, the upper-middle class is still dominated by this race:

> Another thing they have in common is that they are mostly—but not entirely—white. The median Black household had wealth of $3,557 in 2016—down by almost half from 1983. Latinos had $6,591, up a couple thousand dollars. The median white family, on the other hand, had $146,984, up over 80 percent in the same period. People of color are not absent from the top 9.9 percent of the wealth distribution, to be sure—a fact that is central to our collective self-image. It's just that white people are eight times more likely to make it into those happy percentiles. (7)

Even with all of the claims to desire a more diverse and equal society, white privilege is alive and flourishing in the top 9.9%.[87]

Within the storyline of *The Sopranos*, this relation between race and class is highlighted when Meadow starts to date a mixed-race young man at Columbia University.[88] While Tony openly expresses his racist rejection of this boyfriend, Carmela realizes that she needs to take a neutral stance for the benefit of family peace. However, her tolerance of her husband's intolerance indicates how she lives her life on the level of compromise and contradiction: Like so many elite centrists, she wants to see herself as being a good moral person, but she cannot help profiting from a system of inequality and segregation.[89] One of the main

24 *The Sopranos*

ways her complicity with the system is presented is through her efforts to buy a new home in a better neighborhood. As Stewart documents, this focus on home ownership represents the major way that the 9.9% enhances their wealth and increases inequality:

> Homeownership is another feather in the cap of those who succeed in the 9.9 percent game. While the median homeowner has a net worth of $195,400, the median renter has $5,400. That's not just because rich people buy homes; it's because buying (the right) home makes people rich. Some research suggests that homeownership has become such a central part of wealth formation that it may account for most of the increase in wealth inequality. (8)

Although it may not be clear why Carmela continues to invest in real estate, what is evident is that she uses her economic advantages to enhance her wealth and differentiate herself from others.[90] Similar to the way that prestige TV has to market its value by devaluing the competition, Carmela's taste and consumer choices are often centered on signaling her privilege as she outcompetes and devalues others.

Stewart believes that inequality itself undermines reason and makes people act and think in an irrational and counter-productive manner:

> Now, we all know that human beings have always been unreasonable to some degree. They routinely draw conclusions about the way the world is from the way they wish it to be; they systematically overvalue evidence of recent experience and undervalue evidence that comes from far away; they are really bad at math, especially the math of risks and probabilities; they think their team is always in the right, and the other guys are always in the wrong; and so on. As inequality rises, however, all of these cognitive defects become catastrophically worse, or so I show. The human faculties of moral cognition are simply not built to work under conditions of extreme inequality. Even more important, inequality brings forth social forces with the means and the motive to amplify and exploit the growing vulnerabilities in the human cognitive apparatus. This self-combustion of reason, I think, is the real backstory behind the rise of the 9.9 percent. (20)

To this relation between inequality and irrationality, I am adding the way that a certain type of psychopathology and political ideology functions to repress the awareness of negative personal and social effects through a process of narcissistic repression. In terms of prestige TV, this narcissism is centered on aesthetic devices that enable the audience to identify with anti-social behavior and to deny that identification at the same time. In the quest to see ourselves as being good and innocent, we want to have our virtues recognized by others, but this implies repressing our illicit thoughts and desires. We then turn to cultural fantasies to deny what we want as we signal our conformity to elite standards.

As we shall see throughout this book, the main characters of prestige TV shows often embody moral ambiguity and complexity, but their underlying psychology is driven by the pursuit of the pleasure principle. While this type of borderline personality occurs throughout culture and history, what is important to highlight is the way that global capitalism and Neoliberal politics helps to enable the dominance of this psychopathology. Moreover, as I have shown in my analysis of *The Sopranos* and the cultural discourse surrounding the production of prestige TV, Right-wing fantasies are produced and consumed by a mostly "liberal" upper-middle class structured by obsessional narcissism. Even when these shows are streamed by a global audience with a more diverse cultural and economic demographic, the same ironic divide between moral posturing and anti-social desire is evident. It is one of the goals of this work to expose this underlying psychopathology in order to help us think more clearly about the anti-social aspects of centrist politics and subjectivity.

Notes

1 Doucette, Jamie, and Seung-Ook Lee. "Trump, turbulence, territory." *Political Geography* (2019). https://doi.org/10.1016/j.polgeo.2019.02.006
2 Goode, Erich, and D. Angus Vail, eds. *Extreme deviance*. Pine Forge Press, 2008.
3 Poniewozik, James. *Audience of one: Donald Trump, television, and the fracturing of America.* Liveright Publishing, 2019.
4 Pickard, Victor. "Media failures in the age of Trump." *The Political Economy of Communication* 4.2 (2017): 118–122.
5 Laplanche, Jean, and J.- B. Pontalis. "Fantasy and the origins of sexuality." *International Journal of Psycho-Analysis* 49 (1968): 1–18.
6 Freud, Sigmund. "Creative writers and daydreaming." *Standard Edition* 9 (1921): 143–153; "Group psychology and the analysis of the ego." *Standard Edition* 18 (1925): 65–143.
7 Freud, Sigmund. "Repression." *The Psychoanalytic Review (1913–1957)* 9 (1922): 444.
8 Freud, Sigmund. *The interpretation of dreams: the complete and definitive text*. Basic Books, 2010.
9 Freud, Sigmund. "Project for a scientific psychology (1950 [1895])." *The Standard Edition of the complete psychological works of Sigmund Freud, Volume I (1886–1899): pre-psycho-analytic publications and unpublished drafts.* 1966. 281–391.
10 Freud, Sigmund. *Jokes and their relation to the unconscious*. W. W. Norton & Company, 1960.
11 Samuels, Robert. "Catharsis: the politics of enjoyment." *Zizek and the rhetorical unconscious.* Palgrave Macmillan, Cham, 2020. 7–31.
12 Samuels, Robert. *Generation X and the rise of the entertainment subject*. Rowman & Littlefield, 2021.
13 Žižek, Slavoj. *The plague of fantasies*. Verso, 1997.
14 Samuels, Robert. *The psychopathology of political ideologies*. Routledge, 2021.
15 Samuels, Robert. "On the psychopathology of the new right: from Jurassic Park to the gendered culture wars." *New media, cultural studies, and critical theory after postmodernism.* Palgrave Macmillan, New York, 2009. 87–103.
16 Nochimson, Martha P. "David Chase, The Sopranos." *Television Rewired*. University of Texas Press, 2021. 62–90.
17 Soprano, Tony. "Tony Soprano." *The American Villain: Encyclopedia of Bad Guys in Comics, Film, and Television* (2020): 309.
18 Martin, Brett. *Difficult men: behind the scenes of a creative revolution: from The Sopranos and The Wire to Mad Men and Breaking Bad*. Penguin, 2013.

19 McClary, Susan. "Soprano masculinities." *Masculinity in Opera* 3350 (2013).
20 Marx, Karl, and Friedrich Engels. *The communist manifesto.* Yale University Press, 2012.
21 Faludi, Susan. *Backlash: the undeclared war against American women.* Crown, 2009.
22 Lyons, Siobhan. "The (anti-) hero with a thousand faces: reconstructing villainy in The Sopranos, Breaking Bad, and Better Call Saul. "*Canadian Review of American Studies* 51.3 (2021): 225–246.
23 Beale, James. *"The strong, silent type": Tony Soprano, Don Draper, and the construction of the white male antihero in contemporary television drama.* Diss. Bowling Green State University, 2014.
24 Thorburn, David. "The single-series monograph: a new approach to TV studies." *Cinema Journal* 50.4 (2011): 194–201.
25 Root, Wayne Allyn. *Angry white male: how the Donald Trump phenomenon is changing America—and what we can all do to save the middle class.* Simon and Schuster, 2016.
26 Samuels, Robert. "Transference and narcissism." *Freud for the twenty-first century.* Palgrave Pivot, Cham, 2019. 43–51.
27 Samuels, Robert. "Beyond Hillary Clinton: obsessional narcissism and the failure of the liberal class." *Psychoanalyzing the Left and Right after Donald Trump.* Palgrave Macmillan, Cham, 2016. 31–59.
28 Wilson, Rick. *Running against the devil: a plot to save America from Trump—and Democrats from themselves.* Crown Forum, 2020.
29 Klein, Ezra. *Why we're polarized.* Simon and Schuster, 2020.
30 Chambers, John R., Barry R. Schlenker, and Brian Collisson. "Ideology and prejudice: the role of value conflicts." *Psychological Science* 24.2 (2013): 140–149.
31 Denker, Angela. *Red State Christians: understanding the voters who elected Donald Trump.* Fortress Press, 2019.
32 Samuels, Robert. "Simon Clarke and the politics and psychoanalysis of racism." *Psychoanalysis, Culture & Society* 25.1 (2020): 96–100.
33 Frank, Thomas. *Listen, liberal: or, what ever happened to the party of the people?.* Macmillan, 2016.
34 Formisano, Ronald P. *Plutocracy in America: how increasing inequality destroys the middle class and exploits the poor.* JHU Press, 2015.
35 Dark, Taylor E. *The unions and the democrats.* Cornell University Press, 2018.
36 Slaughter, Matthew J. "Globalization and declining unionization in the United States." *Industrial Relations: A Journal of Economy and Society* 46.2 (2007): 329–346.
37 Hedges, Chris. *Death of the liberal class.* Vintage Books Canada, 2011.
38 Marsh, John. *Class dismissed: why we cannot teach or learn our way out of inequality.* NYU Press, 2011.
39 Harris, Adam. "America is divided by education." *The Atlantic* 7 (2018).
40 Wimberly, Cory. "Trump, propaganda, and the politics of ressentiment." *JSP: Journal of Speculative Philosophy* 32.1 (2018): 179–199.
41 Jameson, Frederic. "History and class consciousness as an 'unfinished project'." *The Feminist Standpoint Theory Reader: Intellectual and Political Controversies* 1 (2004): 49–72.
42 Senior, Jordan. *Walk like a man: hegemonic masculinity and un-made men in "The Sopranos."* Diss. University of Huddersfield, 2017.
43 Jubin, Olivier. "Patriarchal (and post-patriarchal) anxiety: the identity dilemmas of a godfather in The Sopranos." *Societes* 2 (2015): 31–42.
44 Gregersdotter, Katarina, and Nicklas Hållén. "Made men and constructed masculinities: viewing the father-son relationship in The Sopranos." *Masculinity/femininty: re-framing a fragmented debate.* Brill, 2012. 29–36.
45 Wilson, Niki Caputo. *The Intersection of gender and Italian/Americaness: hegemony in The Sopranos.* Diss. Florida Atlantic University, 2010.
46 Roberts, Ron. *Psychology and capitalism: the manipulation of mind.* John Hunt Publishing, 2015.

47 Jacobs, Jason. *Violence and therapy in The Sopranos*. Edinburgh University Press, Edinburgh. 2005.

48 Mattessi, Peter. "The strong, silent type: psychoanalysis in The Sopranos." *Metro Magazine: Media & Education Magazine* 138 (2003): 136–138.

49 Mattessi, Peter. "The strong, silent type: psychoanalysis in The Sopranos." *Metro Magazine: Media & Education Magazine* 138 (2003): 136–138.

50 Brod, Harry. "The Sorry Sons of The Godfather: intertextuality, orality and diminished masculinities in The Sopranos." *UNIversitas: Journal of Research, Scholarship, and Creative Activity* 2.2 (2006): 1–6.

51 Gething, Anna. "'A Caligula-like despot': Matriarchal Tyranny in The Sopranos." *Women on screen*. Palgrave Macmillan, London, 2011. 213–224.

52 Quinn, Roseanne Giannini. "Mothers, molls, and misogynists: resisting Italian American womanhood in The Sopranos." *The Journal of American Culture* 27.2 (2004): 166.

53 Freud, Sigmund. *Leonardo da Vinci and a memory of his childhood*. W. W. Norton & Company, 1964.

54 Fiorina, Morris P., Samuel J. Abrams, and Jeremy C. Pope. "Culture war." *The myth of a polarized America*. Longman, 2005.

55 Banet-Weiser, Sarah. "'Ruined' lives: Mediated white male victimhood." *European Journal of Cultural Studies* 24.1 (2021): 60–80.

56 Pagden, Anthony. *The enlightenment: and why it still matters*. Oxford University Press, 2013.

57 Henrich, Joseph. *The WEIRDest people in the world: how the West became psychologically peculiar and particularly prosperous*. Penguin UK, 2020.

58 Rauch, Jonathan. *The constitution of knowledge: a defense of truth*. Brookings Institution Press, 2021.

59 Ridley, Matt. "The rational optimist: how prosperity evolves." *Brock Education Journal* 21.2 (2012): 102–106.

60 DiAngelo, Robin. *White fragility: why it's so hard for white people to talk about racism*. Beacon Press, 2018.

61 Rasmussen, Mikkel Bolt. *Trump's counter-revolution*. John Hunt Publishing, 2018.

62 Ekins, Emily. "Religious Trump voters." *How faith moderates attitudes about immigration, race, and identity. Washington, DC: Democracy and Voter Study Group, Available online:* https://www.cato.org/publications/public-opinion-brief/religioustrump-voters-how-faith-moderates-attitudes-about *(accessed on 5 April 2021)* (2018).

63 Frank, Thomas. *What's the matter with Kansas?: How conservatives won the heart of America*. Picador, 2007.

64 Frank, Thomas. *Pity the billionaire: the hard-times swindle and the unlikely comeback of the right*. Macmillan, 2012.

65 Samuels, Robert. "Trump and Sanders on the Couch: neoliberal populism on the Left and the Right." *Psychoanalyzing the Left and Right after Donald Trump*. Palgrave Macmillan, Cham, 2016. 61–76.

66 Bartlett, Bruce. "Donald Trump and 'Reverse Racism'." *Available at SSRN 2726413* (2016).

67 Moxley Rouse, Carolyn. "Liberal bias: the new 'reverse racism' in the trump era." *American Anthropologist* 121.1 (2019): 172–176.

68 Kelly, Lisa W. "'Authentic' men and 'angry' women: Trump, reality television, and gendered constructions of business and politics." *Trump's Media War*. Palgrave Macmillan, Cham, 2019. 87–99.

69 Finley, Laura, and Luigi Esposito. "The immigrant as bogeyman: examining Donald Trump and the right's anti-immigrant, anti-PC rhetoric." *Humanity & Society* 44.2 (2020): 178–197.

70 Poniewozik, James. *Audience of one: Donald Trump, television, and the fracturing of America*. Liveright Publishing, 2019.

71 Jaramillo, Deborah L. "The family racket: AOL Time Warner, HBO, The Sopranos, and the construction of a quality brand." *Journal of Communication Inquiry* 26.1 (2002): 59–75.

72 Sepinwall, Alan. *The revolution was televised: the cops, crooks, slingers, and slayers who changed TV drama forever.* Simon and Schuster, 2013.

73 Freud, Sigmund. "Notes upon a case of obsessional neurosis." *The Standard Edition of the complete psychological works of Sigmund Freud, Volume X (1909): two case histories ('Little Hans' and the 'Rat Man').* 1955. 151–318.

74 Toscano, Aaron A. "Tony Soprano as the American Everyman and Scoundrel: how The Sopranos (re) presents contemporary middle-class anxieties." *The Journal of Popular Culture* 47.3 (2014): 451–469.

75 Karpf, David. "Digital politics after Trump." *Annals of the International Communication Association* 41.2 (2017): 198–207.

76 Newman, Michael Z., and Elana Levine. *Legitimating television: media convergence and cultural status.* Routledge, 2012.

77 Jaramillo, Deborah L. "The family racket: AOL Time Warner, HBO, The Sopranos, and the construction of a quality brand." *Journal of Communication Inquiry* 26.1 (2002): 59–75.

78 Nutini, Hugo G., and Barry L. Isaac. "Four: the upper classes Aristocracy, Plutocracy, political class, and prestige upper-middle class." *Social stratification in Central Mexico, 1500–2000.* University of Texas Press, 2021. 97–122.

79 Douthat, Ross. "Does meritocracy work?." *Atlantic Monthly* 296.4 (2005): 120.

80 McCabe, Janet, and Kim Akass. *It's not TV, it's HBO's original programming: producing quality TV.* Routledge, 2009.

81 Miller, Brian. "A McMansion for the suburban mob family: the unfulfilling single-family home of The Sopranos." *Journal of Popular Film and Television* 46.4 (2018): 207–218.

82 Stewart, Matthew. *The 9.9%.* Simon and Schuster, 2021.

83 Gregersdotter, Katarina, and Nicklas Hållén. "Made men and constructed masculinities: viewing the father-son relationship in The Sopranos." *Masculinity/femininty: re-framing a fragmented debate.* Brill, 2012. 29–36.

84 Ostrom, Elinor. "Tragedy of the commons." *The New Palgrave Dictionary of Economics* 2. Palgrave, 2008). 1–5.

85 Samuels, Robert. *Educating inequality: beyond the political myths of higher education and the job market.* Routledge, 2017.

86 Wilson, Graeme. "Television antiheroines: women behaving badly in crime and prison drama." *Critical Studies in Media Communication* 34.5 (2017): 509–510.

87 Crozier, Gill. "Race and education: meritocracy as white middle class privilege." *British Journal of Sociology of Education* 39.8 (2018): 1239–1246.

88 Maucione, Jessica. "The revelatory racial politics of The Sopranos: black and brown bodies and storylines as props and backdrop in the normalization of whiteness." *Violence against black bodies.* Routledge, 2017. 127–144.

89 Kelly, Robert J., and Kim C. Francis. "Heartbreakers and bonebreakers: women in the underworld." *Journal of Social Distress and The Homeless* 15.2 (2006): 59–97.

90 Betancourt, Andree EC. "All about my HBO mothers: talking back to Carmela Soprano and Ruth Fisher." *Television and the Self: Knowledge, Identity, and Media Representation.* Lexington Books, 2013: 63.

3

BREAKING BAD

From Walter White to the Alt-Right

While Tony Soprano helps us fantasize about being free from social constraint, *Breaking Bad* depicts the pleasure and destructiveness of compulsive capitalism during a time of failed liberal institutions.[1] On the most basic level, Walter White turns into a sociopathic criminal because not only does he need to pay for expensive healthcare, but he also starts to enjoy the power and freedom he gains from his transgressive activities.[2] Driven by the compulsion to always make more money, Walter exposes a new mode of libertarian survivalism under the cover of being a good family man.[3]

The Political Plot

When the series begins, Walter is a middle-aged, middle-class high school chemistry teacher who discovers that he has lung cancer and no acceptable way of paying for his healthcare. Like so many other Americans, he is victimized by a system that replaces care with a drive for maximum profit; however, his response to this social and political problem is to focus on his own needs and desires as he seeks to access more money at any cost.[4] Although much of the audience's fascination with his character can be connected to his ability to live out fantasies of freedom, wealth, pleasure, and power, the political and economic context of his criminality should not be ignored.[5]

While it is clear that Republicans have helped to produce the costly American healthcare system, what is often misunderstood is how Democrats have also contributed to the transformation of care into profit.[6] Not only was Obama's Affordable Care Act based on a Republican plan, but much of the resistance to making American healthcare more affordable and accessible has been driven by "liberal" professionals who place their own careers over the public good.[7] As one of the main supporters of the Democratic Party, upper-middle-class professionals

DOI: 10.4324/9781003352600-3

30 *Breaking Bad*

represent what has been called the new professional class.[8] According to Matthew Stewart, the people who really shape our culture and institutions are upper-middle-class professionals, who are also the main targets for prestige TV shows.[9] These are the people who have been able to take advantage of our unequal society by making a rigged system work to their benefit. For instance, while higher education has become more expensive and exclusive, professional elites have learned how to help their children out-compete others in a war of competitive advantages.[10] Although these elites may say that they are for a more diverse and equal society, many of their actions are centered on a survivalist mentality as they seek to maintain and increase their wealth, power, and prestige.

As Stewart documents, between 1963 and 2016, 90% of Americans saw their relative wealth decline (6). While the rich have gotten richer, most others have had their wages and wealth stagnate as the cost of housing, college, and healthcare have risen dramatically. At the same time, the job market has increasingly rewarded people with college diplomas, with most of the rewards going to individuals with professional degrees.[11] Higher education, therefore, has not made society more equal and mobile, which are the goals of a modern liberal democracy; instead, these institutions cater to the wealthy and often place the unwealthy in debt.[12]

In many ways, the rigging of higher education for the wealthy has been a bi-partisan affair, but what is often not noticed is how these "liberal" institutions produce the very inequality they protest against.[13] For example, most of the faculty in higher education now do not have job security or earn a livable wage.[14] Progressive professors tend to blame this problem on evil administrators or cost-cutting state legislatures, and yet, much of the inequality is driven by the elite tenured professors who profit from a system of labor exploitation.[15] The same faculty who critique inequality and prejudice are committed to a system obsessed by ranking, rating, and grading everything.[16] Through a focus on their individual careers, these faculty members have tried to hide their investment in power, profit, and prestige behind the values of liberal democracy. Even when they try to signal their virtue by attacking racism, sexism, and homophobia, what they are often doing is trying to cover their own guilt and shame through public acts of cultural morality.[17]

At the heart of the Democratic Party, we find the same dynamic that combines a moral call for increased equality and justice with a commitment to profiting from an unequal system.[18] In this structure, the people who gain the most from inequality and social hierarchy pretend to be the ones fighting against poverty and inequality, and one of the main ways that they hide their own hypocrisy and complicity is by turning to the myth of meritocratic individualism.[19] According to this shared cultural fantasy, if a person works hard and plays by the rules, their talent and knowledge will be recognized and rewarded. The secret to this ideology is that it places all of the credit and blame on the isolated, competitive individual, which feeds a destructive form of anti-social capitalism.[20]

The ideology of meritocratic individualism is also depicted in prestige TV shows that seek to represent social issues through the stories of particular characters. For example, in *Breaking Bad*, the harmful nature of the American healthcare and educational labor system is depicted through the trials and tribulations of a fictionalized character, Walter White.[21] Since he does not want to ask anyone else to help him pay for the high costs of his medical treatment, and his job as a high school teacher does not pay him enough, he is forced into a life of crime, which he then grows to enjoy.[22] The show itself does nothing to help us understand or change the destructive American healthcare system; rather, it focuses on how an individual attempts to survive in a highly unequal, profit-driven world.

Media Crime Culture

In analyzing *Breaking Bad*, what is often missed is how Walter's initial interest in turning to a life of crime is first triggered when he watches on television the results of a drug bust.[23] He is fascinated by the amount of money that was recovered, and he begins to ask his brother-in-law, Hank, who works in law enforcement, about how much one can make by selling drugs. By tracing the origins of his life of crime to an event depicted on a television screen, the show makes an ironic reflection on its own representation of criminality.[24] Just as the audience is watching the drive to make money through crime, Walter himself is also watching with the same fascination. The shown then becomes doubled as it both represents the unfolding of the plot *and* depicts the way the media affects the audience. Moreover, since it is Walter who is the viewer of the television show, he becomes a representation of the audience itself. It is then not only that we may sympathize with the devil, we are also identified with him.[25]

This doubling effect introduces an ironic context where one can be guilty and innocent at the same time since every representation is both stated and placed in quotation marks.[26] In fact, one of the great achievements of the series is that it is able to combine comedy and drama together as a narrative full of suspense and emotional extremes is coupled with an ironic, comedic awareness.[27] As Freud insisted, the power of humor is that it shows the ability of the ego to transform suffering into pleasure and the serious into the unserious as the self triumphs over a harsh reality.[28] The drug that the show then ultimately delivers is the instant access to enjoyment through an escape from the destructiveness of contemporary American society, economics, and politics.[29]

Not only does Walter White produce and distribute meth, but the show itself creates and circulates an escapist version of the present. Prestige TV, then, is the drug of choice for the elites of an ailing society who see no hope for the future and no way of escaping from a destructive capitalist system.[30] Furthermore, by representing the angry white man as a victim who is forced to turn to a life of crime, the show foreshadows and rationalizes the rise to power of anti-social, reactionary capitalists like Donald Trump.[31] The rapacious criminal class is therefore produced and sold from within liberal culture as the only realistic response to a broken social system.

Although Walter White is not a true member of the 9.9%, what he helps to embody is the underlying logic that in an unfair and unequal society, one must focus on the survival of oneself and one's immediate family.[32] From this

32 *Breaking Bad*

perspective, we can see that the failure of Democrats to address issues concerning inequality, education, labor, and healthcare has not only pushed the working class to move over to the Republicans, but the underlying culture and ideology produced and circulated by centrists feeds a Right-wing reactionary discourse and survivalist mentality.[33]

Ironic Awareness

In analyzing this series, it is important to understand how humor, irony, and metafiction create a world that combines immersion with distance, which enables the audience the ability to escape reality from a position of ironic knowingness.[34] The humor of the show, therefore, is not just an added feature but a defining element. Starting with the first scene from the pilot episode, Walter is introduced wearing nothing but his tight, white jockey underpants and a gas mask.[35] This comic depiction is coupled with a display of intense fear. The first question we have to ask is why does the creator of the show begin with such a humorous presentation of the main character?[36]

In the original script for the pilot episode, we find the following description of the opening scene of the series:

> Ducking outside, he starts breathing again. A short sleeve DRESS SHIRT on a hanger dangles from the Winnebago's awning. Underpants pulls it on. He finds a clip-on tie in the pocket, snaps it to his collar. No trousers, unfortunately.
>
> He licks his fingers, slicks his hair down with his hands. He's looking almost pulled together now – at least from the waist-up. All the while, the sirens are getting LOUDER.
>
> Underpants figures out how to turn on the camcorder. He twists the little screen around so he can see himself in it. Framing himself waist-up, he takes a moment to gather his thoughts … then presses RECORD.

Walter is therefore introduced as both a tragic and comic figure as his bottom half is clothed only in his white underpants, whereas he looks more professional and desperate on top.[37] This combination of opposing aesthetic forms allows for the show to be always read on two different levels: on one level, we must take the plot seriously and judge the development of his character through a moral lens, and on another level, we are induced to suspend judgment and laugh at the absurdity of life and the situation.

Walter White, Alt-Right

As the series documents how Walter White becomes an angry white man, it reflects unintentionally the move of the working class from the Democrats to the Republicans. On the most basic level, Walter's transformation is blamed on the combination of high medical costs and a low teacher's salary. Since he cannot take care of himself and he does not want to rely on the charity of others, he seeks out an alternative mode of income. In this context, it is important to realize that the move of frustrated workers from the Democrats to the Republicans concerned mostly white men, and so we have to examine the role that race and gender played in this shift.[38]

Since the Right has used racism and sexism as a way of recruiting angry displaced white working males, cultural representations have played a key role in the political shift between parties.[39] This use of race and gender can be seen in the series as Walter is pitted against Mexican-Americans, foreigners, and women.[40] In most of these cases, he is competing with these minority groups in the drug trade, but in terms of his fight with women, the focus is on his relationship with his wife.[41] As we see in many prestige TV shows, women are often represented as being the ones who stand in the way of the male anti-hero achieving his goals.[42] With *Breaking Bad*, Walter's wife, Skyler, is no exception. Even after he continuously lies to her and basically rapes her, fans still express their dislike for her character.[43]

Depicting as the nagging and controlling wife, Skyler externalizes Walter's super-ego. Thus, while the male protagonist just wants to be free and act on his urges, this woman embodies the social castration and censorship of masculine desire.[44] Although one would think that the audience would side with her, the real support is for the anti-social borderline personality who will do anything to get his way, including killing children and producing a harmful drug. In this defense of the male drive, we see how Freud was correct when he claimed that the active libido is coded as masculine.[45]

As some have pointed out, the more Walter looks like a white supremacist, the more he starts to act as one.[46] It is not that he believes his race is necessarily superior, but he does follow the Right's tendency to associate other races with pure criminality and an animal-like violence.[47] In the first two seasons, this trend is established through his encounter with the Mexican-American drug distributor, Tuco. This crazed, violent man is shot by Walter after he has previously killed another Mexican-American.[48] What, in part, allows the audience not to reject Walter for these violent acts is that they are represented as being justified given the targets.[49] In fact, even Hank, the representation of the law in the series, constantly dehumanizes Mexican-Americans as he calls them "beaners" and sees them as inherently violent and criminal.[50]

Hank also, at times, eggs on Walter and tells him that he needs to wear the pants in the family. By trying to get Walt to become more like a stereotypical aggressive male, we see that his problem is not only his lack of money but also his lack of manliness.[51] What, then, allows him to escape from both of these lacks is his turn to violent crime. In fact, after he sells meth for the first time, he becomes invigorated and starts to touch his wife in a sexual manner under the table during a public meeting.[52] The message here appears to be that by becoming more violent and anti-social, he also becomes more masculine and sexual.

34 *Breaking Bad*

Middle-Class Survivalism

When his family tries to intervene and discover why he has become so secretive and absent, he declares that he never made any choices on his own in his life, and so he now chooses not to go for cancer treatment.[53] His search for freedom and control in an emasculating world is therefore tied to his acceptance of death, and yet, he still wants to earn enough money through his crimes in order to set his family up for a comfortable future. As he calculates how much it will cost to send his kids to college, he depicts the desperate struggle of the former middle class to survive in a highly unequal society. As Christopher Lasch argues in *The Culture of Narcissism*, the poor have always had to struggle for their survival, but now so do the middle class.[54]

Walter then reveals the anxiety that surrounds the disappearing middle class, which has been abandoned by both political parties.[55] While the Right attempts to substitute race and gender conflict for class warfare, we see how the "liberal" media also tends to translate economic issues into personal narratives concerning survival. For Lasch, writing in 1980, driving this survivalist mentality is a sense of doom coupled with a lost faith in modern liberal institutions: "Impending disaster has become an everyday concern, so commonplace and familiar that nobody any longer gives much thought to how disaster might be averted. People busy themselves instead with survival strategies, measures designed to prolong their own lives, or programs guaranteed to ensure good health and peace of mind" (4). Since we no longer believe that we can fix our most pressing problems, all we can do is focus on our own will to survive in a battle of competing individuals.[56]

This type of survivalist competition is presented in *Breaking Bad* through Walter's fight with other drug dealers and criminals. Since he needs to protect his own interests, he finds ways of rationalizing his destructive anti-social behavior.[57] Although the audience can always take comfort in reminding itself that it is watching a fictional representation of an extreme character from the position of ironic distance, Walter's plight reinforces a politics and subjectivity centered on pathological narcissism.[58] In fact, Walter does not just want to make meth to make money; he also wants to be recognized for making the best meth and for doing anything to protect his product.[59] Thus, when he puts on his hat and sunglasses and tells people to call him Heisenberg, he reveals that he is obsessed about how others view him.[60] Within the plot, this desire for recognition is derived in part from the way his early business partners failed to credit him for his contributions to their eventual business and scientific success. He is therefore driven, not only by his need for personal survival or the protection of his family; rather, he wants to be recognized for his expertise and knowledge.

According to Lasch, narcissism and survivalism are tied together because they both represent a focus on the self and a lost belief in social solutions: "survival has become the 'catchword of the seventies' and 'collective narcissism' the dominant disposition. Since 'the society' has no future, it makes sense to live only for the moment, to fix our eyes on our own 'private performance,' to become connoisseurs of our own decadence, to cultivate a 'transcendental self-attention'" (6). In anticipating our contemporary politics and psychology, Lasch reveals a link between psychopathology, ideology, and culture: Starting in the 1970s, a lost belief in liberal democratic social institutions resulted in a focus on the performing self.[61] Of course, social media has only heightened this mode of narcissism, but what should be highlighted is that Lasch connects these social and subjective changes to precisely the period when economic inequality increased and social mobility decreased.[62]

What we find in *Breaking Bad* and *The Culture of Narcissism* is the same coupling of lost belief with an anxious sense of a coming disaster:

> Social conditions today encourage a survival mentality, expressed in its crudest form in disaster movies or in fantasies of space travel, which allow vicarious escape from a doomed planet. People no longer dream of overcoming difficulties but merely of surviving them. In business, according to Jennings, "The struggle is to survive emotionally"—to "preserve or enhance one's identity or ego." The normative concept of developmental stages promotes a view of life as an obstacle course: the aim is simply to get through the course with a minimum of trouble and pain. (49)

This sense that life is an obstacle course that we have to learn how to navigate in order to survive our impending doom describes many of the plots of the prestige TV shows discussed in this book.[63] Furthermore, as we continue to deny climate change and other existential threats because we do not believe we can do anything to reverse our course, we seek fantasized magical escapes delivered by the culture industry.[64]

It is vital to stress that prestige TV both reflects and distorts our political and social order. In fact, we know from research done on how news watching affects people's moods and perceptions of the world that political pathologies are shaped in part by the selective representation of negative, fear-inducing topics.[65] If we extend this analysis of news programs to fictional series like *Breaking Bad*, we can affirm that the constant depiction of crime and other anti-social behaviors makes people paranoid and anxious.[66] Lasch touches on this point in the following passage:

> The ethic of self-preservation and psychic survival is rooted, then, not merely in objective conditions of economic warfare, rising rates of crime, and social chaos but in the subjective experience of emptiness and isolation. It reflects the conviction—as much a projection of inner anxieties as a perception of the way things are—that envy and exploitation dominate even the most intimate relations. (51)

The drive, then, to focus on self-survival is due in part from the combination of isolation and the awareness of real and imagined social threats. Furthermore, the constant depiction of envy and exploitation in the media helps to determine how people see themselves and the world around them.

Lasch adds that many different factors have contributed to the adoption of a survivalist mentality, but in his historical account, he focuses on how the undermining of the "Protestant work ethic" has been a major reason for the lost hope in modern liberal democratic institutions:

> In an age of diminishing expectations, the Protestant virtues no longer excite enthusiasm. Inflation erodes investments and savings. Advertising undermines the horror of indebtedness, exhorting the consumer to buy now and pay later. As the future becomes menacing and uncertain, only fools put off until tomorrow the fun they can have today. A profound shift in our sense of time has transformed work habits, values, and the definition of success. Self-preservation has replaced self-improvement as the goal of earthly existence. In a lawless, violent, and unpredictable society, in which the normal conditions of everyday life come to resemble those formerly confined to the underworld, men live by their wits. (53)

Ironically, Lasch's analysis mimics the way shows like *Breaking Bad* portray current society in such a dark and cynical manner. Although the truth is that crime rates have been going down and violent deaths have also decreased, the media and academic critics tend to present a negative view of the world.[67]

According to Steven Pinker, progressives hate progress because they do not want to admit that the modern liberal institutions of science, democracy, and capitalism have, on average, helped to increase health, living standards, knowledge, and rights on a global level.[68] In terms of the "liberal" media, Pinker bemoans the fact that slow progress is rarely noticed, but according to the news mantra, "if it bleeds, it leads." Since recent threatening events draw our attention more than slow positive successes, the media seeks to cash in on our attention by giving us what it thinks will arouse our interest.[69] Cultural critics and media outlets are then motivated to represent the world in negative, threatening ways.

By watching real and imagined criminality, we lose trust in social institutions while we are taught to adopt a survivalist mode of individualism. Lasch traces this new attitude to a transformation of modern capitalism from one based on hard work and discipline to one centered on immediate consumption: "In earlier times, the self-made man took pride in his judgment of character and probity; today he anxiously scans the faces of his fellows not so as to evaluate their credit but in order to gauge their susceptibility to his own blandishments. He practices the classic arts of seduction and with the same indifference to moral niceties, hoping to win your heart while picking your pocket" (53). Although we should question Lasch's very negative appraisal of post-modern society, his analysis does match the way the world is represented through most prestige TV shows.[70] The question, then, is why an upper-middle-class centrist audience is so hungry to watch these cynical representations.

On the one hand, viewing criminal behavior from the safety of your home serves to contain and control perceived social threats. After all, if you no longer believe in the power of social institutions to protect you, then it makes sense to seek out a way to anticipate and defang threatening elements. On the other hand, watching the representation of a mean, anti-social world makes people more paranoid and socially insecure. Culture, therefore, has to find a way to make people not care about what they are viewing on a conscious level, and this is done through the use of humor, irony, and other aesthetic distancing effects.[71] It is also essential to give people a safe outlet to express their repressed desires and fears, and in the case of narcissistic centrists, the process involves projecting anti-social desires onto a criminal class.[72] This dynamic has the added benefit of allowing the enlightened viewers the ability to mock and laugh at social transgressions.

The audiences' complicity then has to be constantly conjured and then released as they receive the message that their elite viewing habits have no real effect on their values and beliefs.[73] Although Lasch focuses mainly on how the economic system has been the major cause for the change in social subjectivity, I have been arguing that popular culture also has a major effect. Interestingly, Lasch tends to remove culture and cultural criticism from the causes for this transformation to a survivalist mentality:

> The transformation of the myth of success—of the definition of success and of the qualities believed to promote it—is a long-term development arising not from particular historical events but from general changes in the structure of society: the shifting emphasis from capitalist production to consumption; the growth of large organizations and bureaucracies; the increasingly dangerous and warlike conditions of social life. (63)

In stressing the mostly economic causes for social and subjective changes, Lasch leaves out the role played by popular culture, and this is indicative of the centrist desire to repress awareness of the cultural fantasies supporting political ideologies.

Lasch goes as far as saying that the white audience's interest in people of color stems from the way that middle-class life, in general, has taken on the form of the "black ghetto":

> In some ways middle-class society has become a pale copy of the black ghetto, as the appropriation of its language would lead us to believe. We do not need to minimize the poverty of the ghetto or the suffering inflicted by whites on blacks in order to see that the increasingly dangerous and

38 *Breaking Bad*

unpredictable conditions of middle-class life have given rise to similar strategies for survival. Indeed the attraction of black culture for disaffected whites suggests that black culture now speaks to a general condition, the most important feature of which is a widespread loss of confidence in the future. (67–68)

As we shall see in the next chapter on *The Wire*, a key aspect of this "liberal" fantasy world is the representation of people of color as being uncivilized, hyper-sexual, and violent criminals. In the mode of a repressed fantasy, the liberal imagination feeds conservative prejudices and stereotypes.

Notes

1 Conway, Joseph. "From disincorporation to rematerialization: breaking bad and the life of cash." *Canadian Review of American Studies* 51.3 (2021): 196–212.
2 Lee, David R. *What's the matter with Walter? The privatization of everything in Breaking Bad*. Harvard University, 2016.
3 Bohr, Marco, et al. *The interior landscapes of Breaking Bad*. Rowman & Littlefield, 2019.
4 Holland, Jack. "The personal is political (in Breaking Bad)." *Fictional television and American Politics*. Manchester University Press, 2020. 186–201.
5 Bannon, Sam. "Captain America is a meth addict: analyzing Vince Gilligan's subtle and scathing indictment of America in Breaking Bad." *The Mall* 3.1 (2019): 5.
6 Rovner, Julie. "The complicated, political, expensive, seemingly eternal US healthcare debate explained." *BMJ* 367 (2019): https://pubmed.ncbi.nlm.nih.gov/31601555/
7 Lanford, Daniel, and Jill Quadagno. "Implementing ObamaCare: the politics of Medicaid expansion under the Affordable Care Act of 2010." *Sociological Perspectives* 59.3 (2016): 619–639.
8 Mellow, Nicole. "An identity crisis for the Democrats?." *Polity* 52.3 (2020): 324–338.
9 Constantino, Paul R., et al. "The Birth of a New American Aristocracy: In June, Matthew Stewart wrote about the gilded future of the top 10 percent—and the end of opportunity for everyone else." *The Atlantic* 322.2 (2018): 8–10.
10 Rivera, Lauren A. *Pedigree*. Princeton University Press, 2016.
11 Lee, Sang Yoon Tim, Yongseok Shin, and Donghoon Lee. *The option value of human capital: higher education and wage inequality*. No. w21724. National Bureau of Economic Research, 2015.
12 Macy, Anne, and Neil Terry. "The determinants of student college debt." *Southwestern Economic Review* 34 (2007): 15–25.
13 Samuels, Robert. *Educating inequality: beyond the political myths of higher education and the job market*. Routledge, 2017.
14 Schwartz, Joseph M. "Resisting the exploitation of contingent faculty labor in the neoliberal university: the challenge of building solidarity between tenured and non-tenured faculty." *New Political Science* 36.4 (2014): 504–522.
15 Kezar, Adrianna, and Daniel Maxey. "Troubling ethical lapses: the treatment of contingent faculty." *Change: The Magazine of Higher Learning* 46.4 (2014): 34–37.
16 Bousquet, Marc, and Cary Nelson. *How the university works*. New York University Press, 2008.
17 McWhorter, John. "The virtue signalers won't change the world." *The Atlantic* 23 (2018). https://www.theatlantic.com/ideas/archive/2018/12/why-third-wave-anti-racism-dead-end/578764/
18 Hedges, Chris. *Death of the liberal class*. Vintage Books Canada, 2011.
19 Liu, Amy. "Unraveling the myth of meritocracy within the context of US higher education." *Higher education* 62.4 (2011): 383–397.

20 Bloodworth, James. *The myth of meritocracy: why working-class kids still get working-class jobs (provocations series)*. Biteback Publishing, 2016.

21 Brown, Paula. "The American Western Mythology of 'Breaking Bad'." *Studies in Popular Culture* 40.1 (2017): 78–101.

22 Miles, Travis. *Sympathy for the devil: Walter White and a case for the villain's journey*. Truman State University, 2015.

23 Guilfoy, Kevin. "Hatred: Walter White is doing it all wrong." *Philosophy and Breaking Bad*. Palgrave Macmillan, Cham, 2017. 201–216.

24 Cowlishaw, Bridget Roussell, ed. *Masculinity in Breaking Bad: critical perspectives*. McFarland, 2015.

25 Kjeldgaard-Christiansen, Jens. "The bad breaks of Walter White: an evolutionary approach to the fictional antihero." *Evolutionary Studies in Imaginative Culture* 1.1 (2017): 103–120.

26 Perkins, Robert L., ed. *The concept of irony*. Vol. 2. Mercer University Press, 2001.

27 Havas, Julia, and Maria Sulimma. "Through the gaps of my fingers: genre, femininity, and cringe aesthetics in dramedy television." *Television & New Media* 21.1 (2020): 75–94.

28 Freud, S. "Humor. Standard edition, Vol. 21." *London: Ho* (1927): 160–167.

29 Samuels, Robert. "Catharsis: The politics of enjoyment." *Zizek and the rhetorical unconscious*. Palgrave Macmillan, Cham, 2020. 7–31.

30 Fisher, Mark. *Capitalist realism: is there no alternative?*. John Hunt Publishing, 2009.

31 Wilson, Graeme John. *Angry White Men: How Breaking Bad and The Walking Dead Predicted the Trumpian Zeitgeist*. Diss. Bowling Green State University, 2019.

32 Kjeldgaard-Christiansen, Jens. "The bad breaks of Walter White: An evolutionary approach to the fictional antihero." *Evolutionary Studies in Imaginative Culture* 1.1 (2017): 103–120.

33 Kimmel, Michael, and Abby L. Ferber. "'White men are this nation': Right-Wing Militias and the restoration of rural American masculinity." *Rural sociology* 65.4 (2000): 582–604.

34 Kimmel, Michael, and Abby L. Ferber. "'White men are this nation': Right-Wing Militias and the restoration of rural American masculinity." *Rural sociology* 65.4 (2000): 582–604.

35 "Pilot." Breaking Bad. Written by Vince Gilligan, season 1, Sony Pictures, 2008. Von Ancken, David, director.

36 San Juan, Eric. *Breaking down Breaking Bad: unpeeling the layers of Television's greatest drama*. Lulu. com, 2013.

37 Johnson, Paul Elliott. "Walter White (ness) lashes out: Breaking Bad and male victimage." *Critical Studies in Media Communication* 34.1 (2017): 14–28.

38 Carnes, Nicholas, and Noam Lupu. "The white working class and the 2016 election." *Perspectives on Politics* 19.1 (2021): 55–72.

39 Prasad, Monica, Steve G. Hoffman, and Kieran Bezila. "Walking the line: the white working class and the economic consequences of morality." *Politics & Society* 44.2 (2016): 281–304.

40 Johnson, Paul Elliott. "Walter White (ness) lashes out: Breaking Bad and male victimage." *Critical Studies in Media Communication* 34.1 (2017): 14–28.

41 Mittell, Jason. "Lengthy interactions with hideous men: Walter White and the serial poetics of television anti-heroes." *Storytelling in the media convergence age*. Palgrave Macmillan, London, 2015. 74–92.

42 Parunov, Pavao. "Chapter six anti-hero masculinity in television narratives: the example of Breaking Bad's Walter White." Ed. Michael Brennan. *Theorising the Popular* (2017): 104.

43 Holladay, Holly Willson, and Melissa A. Click. "Hating Skyler White." *Anti-Fandom: Dislike and Hate in the Digital Age* 24 (2019): 147.

44 Cowlishaw, Bridget Roussell, ed. *Masculinity in Breaking Bad: critical perspectives*. McFarland, 2015.

45 Freud, Sigmund. *On narcissism: an introduction.* Read Books Ltd, 2014.

46 Hargraves, Hunter. "Of handmaids and men." *Communication Culture & Critique* 11.1 (2018): 189–191.

47 Hutchinson, Darren Lenard. "Continually reminded of their inferior position: social dominance, implicit bias, criminality, and race." *Wash. UJL & Pol'y* 46 (2014): 23.

48 Ruiz, Jason. "Dark matters: Vince Gilligan's Breaking Bad, suburban crime dramas, and Latinidad in the golden age of cable television." *Aztlan: A Journal of Chicano Studies* 40.1 (2015): 37–62.

49 Mittell, Jason. "Lengthy interactions with hideous men: Walter White and the serial poetics of television anti-heroes." *Storytelling in the media convergence age.* Palgrave Macmillan, London, 2015. 74–92.

50 McDonough, Matthew. "Breaking Bad and the intersection of critical theory at race, disability, and gender." (2020): http://hdl.handle.net/20.500.12648/1578

51 White, Walter. "Family man." *Masculinity in Breaking Bad: Critical Perspectives* (2015): 13.

52 Mittell, Jason. "Lengthy interactions with hideous men: Walter White and the serial poetics of television anti-heroes." *Storytelling in the media convergence age.* Palgrave Macmillan, London, 2015. 74–92.

53 Aarons, Leslie A. "The transformation of Walter White: a case study in Bad Faith." *Philosophy and Breaking Bad.* Palgrave Macmillan, Cham, 2017. 175–189.

54 Lasch, Christopher. *The culture of narcissism: American life in an age of diminishing expectations.* W. W. Norton & Company, 2018.

55 Lazonick, William. "Labor in the twenty-first century: the top 0.1% and the disappearing middle-class." *Institute for New Economic Thinking Working Paper Series* 4 (2015).

56 Brunila, Kristiina. "The rise of the survival discourse in an era of therapisation and neoliberalism." *Education Inquiry* 5.1 (2014): 24044.

57 Guilfoy, Kevin. "Hatred: Walter White is doing it all wrong." *Philosophy and Breaking Bad.* Palgrave Macmillan, Cham, 2017. 201–216.

58 Bergquist, Emma D. "The best in every way: a clinical diagnosis of Walter White." *The Mall* 5.1 (2021): 18.

59 Fahy, Declan. "The chemist as anti-hero: Walter White and Sherlock Holmes as case studies." *Hollywood chemistry: when science met entertainment.* American Chemical Society. EDS. Nelson, J. Paglia, S. Perkowitz and K. Grazier, K. 2013. 175–188.

60 Echart, Pablo. "Breaking Bad: an evil self-assertion at life's Twilight." *Framing the Apocalypse.* Eds. Sheila C. Bibb and Alexandra Simon-López. Brill, 2015. 143–166.

61 Borstelmann, Thomas. *The 1970s: a new global history from civil rights to economic inequality.* Vol. 8. Princeton University Press, 2013.

62 Mishel, Lawrence. *Causes of wage stagnation.* Washington, DC: Economic Policy Institute, 2015.

63 Charpentier, Anton. *Neoliberalism in prestige television: a story of masculinity, gender, and finance.* Diss. University of Calgary, 2021.

64 Katz, Elihu, and David Foulkes. "On the use of the mass media as 'escape': clarification of a concept." *Public Opinion Quarterly* 26.3 (1962): 377–388.

65 Bilandzic, Helena, and Patrick Rössler. "Life according to television. Implications of genre-specific cultivation effects: the gratification/cultivation model." *Communications*, Vol. 29, (2004): 295–326.

66 Eschholz, Sarah, Ted Chiricos, and Marc Gertz. "Television and fear of crime: program types, audience traits, and the mediating effect of perceived neighborhood racial composition." *Social Problems* 50.3 (2003): 395–415.

67 Gerbner, George, et al. "The mean world syndrome: media violence & the cultivation of fear." *Media Education Foundation documentary transcript* [http://www. mediaed. org/transcripts/Mean-World-Syndrome-Transcript. pdf] 19 (2010): 2020.

68 Pinker, Steven. *Enlightenment now: the case for reason, science, humanism, and progress.* Penguin UK, 2018.

69 Weitzer, Ronald, and Charis E. Kubrin. "Breaking news: how local TV news and real-world conditions affect fear of crime." *Justice Quarterly* 21.3 (2004): 497–520.

70 Sennett, Richard. *The fall of public man.* W. W. Norton & Company, 2017.

71 Baudrillard, Jean. *The transparency of evil: essays on extreme phenomena.* Verso, 1993.

72 George, Sheldon, and Derek Hook, eds. *Lacan and race: racism, identity, and psychoanalytic theory.* Routledge, 2021.

73 Knobloch-Westerwick, Silvia, Matthias R. Hastall, and Maik Rossmann. "Coping or escaping? Effects of life dissatisfaction on selective exposure." *Communication Research* 36.2 (2009): 207–228.

4

THE WIRE AND THE DEATH OF LIBERAL INSTITUTIONS

As another example of prestige TV and gritty realism, HBO's *The Wire* focuses on how a single urban center has been reshaped by the combination of drugs and failed social institutions.[1] In centering this series in a Democratic city, the program reveals another way that the Democratic Party has failed to protect its constituents as it also presents a cultural fantasy of African-American sex and violence for the pleasure of a white, upper-middle-class "liberal" audience.[2] In showing the failures of the legal system, the education system, the unions, and journalism, the program depicts what Chris Hedges has labeled *The Death of the Liberal Class*.[3]

The Democratic City

A political truism today is that urban centers in America have a high number of minorities who support the Democratic Party, but these same places are often the one's with the highest crime and incarceration rates.[4] In cities like Detroit, Chicago, Baltimore, and Los Angeles, the Democratic machine watches over a populace decimated by job loss, drugs, and endemic racism.[5] While Right-wing politicians like to point to a failure of "Liberal" policies, it is important to understand how popular culture mediates politics and our perceptions of political ideologies.[6] On one level, it is true that Democratic policies have failed to protect the working class and a diverse range of minority groups at the same time that the party represents itself as the champion of these interests.[7] However, the Republican Party has also failed to protect these groups as it has translated a mostly economic conflict into a culture war.[8] Moreover, as the Left tends to focus on gender and race and not class, centrists often signal their virtue by pretending to care about racism and sexism as they ignore most economic problems.[9]

From Hedge's perspective, driving the fall of the liberal class is a focus on careerism over concern for the public good. To prove this point, he documents

DOI: 10.4324/9781003352600-4

The Wire and the Death of Liberal Institutions **43**

how unions, universities, newspapers, and political parties have all been restructured and undermined by a careerist, professional mentality that turns public institutions into systems catering to the individual pursuit of pleasure, profit, and prestige.[10] Thus, instead of faculty at universities trying to help make the populace more educated and democratic, professors concentrate on enhancing their reputations and compensation.[11] Likewise, journalist no longer seek to discover and present the unvarnished truth; instead, they desire to build their careers by becoming entertainers and celebrities.[12] In the case of unions, Hedges finds a similar focus on careerism in both the people running these organizations and the ones they are seeking to represent.[13] At the same time, political parties have become restructured by the single drive for individuals to get elected and re-elected. For example, members of Congress spend much of their time soliciting campaign contributions and then meeting with donors.[14]

In the first season of *The Wire*, the degradation of these liberal institutions is depicted through a failed war on drugs. As a direct indictment of the liberal class, the writers depict an African-American state senator who receives regular campaign contributions from a drug gang.[15] In fact, this corrupt Democrat also undermines the police who are trying to expose the inner-working of the drug trade as he pressures the leaders of law enforcement to end their investigation so that he can continue to receive his money.[16] In this circle of corruption, the Democratic Party feeds off of the money that they receive from the criminal class as they work to undermine the attempts of law enforcement to protect citizens.[17]

Within the context of the show, as mostly African-American drug gangs cater to predominantly African-American drug users, the destructive aspects of the drug trade and the drug war are revealed.[18] While this focus on people of color may be a direct reflection of the actual reality on the ground, the transformation of this actuality for the purposes of entertainment shows how a mode of journalism has itself become a product of the culture industry.[19] Furthermore, the series feeds the conservative racist association between blackness and criminality as it both highlights and produces a lack of social trust in liberal institutions.[20]

What is often missed in the analysis of this series is the way it combines liberal journalism and the entertainment industry. From the perspective of modern liberal democracy, there should be a clear separation between reporting the news as a public good and the use of fictional representations to provide pleasure and make money.[21] Journalism should be centered on discovering and representing the truth, while entertainment is focused on providing enjoyment and escape. However, due in part to the confusion between journalism and entertainment, not only do people not know what to believe but the very foundations of liberal culture are undermined.

Whereas liberal journalism relies on fact-checking and a clear editorial process, the culture industry does not have to get its facts right as it mostly serves as an escape from reality.[22] Thus, even when a show like *The Wire* does try to depict aspects of urban reality in contemporary American life, its use of fictional characters undermines our sense of what is real and not real. Ultimately, this blurring of the distinction between fact and fiction contributes to the loss of trust in liberal social institutions.[23]

The death of the liberal class is also documented in this series through its depiction of main protagonist, McNulty, whose dogged search for the truth could help to restore our lost faith in the legal and law enforcement systems; however, McNulty's is portrayed as a deeply flawed character who is often drinking on and off the job as he tends to take the law into his own hands.[24] This representation of a prestige TV anti-hero is in part motivated out of the need to show how the system itself is rigged and corrupt, and so it can only be saved by an individual who is willing to bend the rules.[25] As the series exposes the failures of the legal system, it motivates the angry white male to seek justice on his own.[26]

Centrist Racism Incorporated

Underlying this depiction of the failed liberal state, we find the production of a centrist form of racism. Since the centrist obsessional narcissist wants to be seen as being progressive, anti-social sexual and violent drives have to be repressed and often projected onto dark others who are then idealized for their access to uncivilized freedom and enjoyment.[27] In this "liberal" mode of racism, people of color are not demonized because they are seen as inferior; rather, the dark other is idealized for their lack of castration and censorship.[28]

Due to the fact that the show originally catered to a mostly white, affluent audience, it feeds the structure of racist fantasies and idealizations that unintentionally furthers the cause of conservative and Right-wing racism.[29] Even if the writers of the series insist that they are just documenting the truth of this inner-city reality, their use of fictional elements and narrative devices serves to select and repress specific aspects of the complex truth.[30] Just as individuals construct stories to convince themselves that they are good and righteous, creators of TV shows produce an edited form of reality from the position of the one who knows. In fact, the idea of "the wire" in the title of the show points to the role of surveillance in contemporary society, where technology allows people to know things they could not know in the past.[31]

Not only after 9/11 did the government start to use different surveillance technologies to spy on its own citizens like never before, but new modes of social media heighten a sense that the modern liberal distinction between the public and the private realms has been eroded.[32] As people turn to new media technologies to render their private lives more public, public institutions have been privatized. Furthermore, the cultural industry feeds off of exposing the private lives of public officials, and this form of surveillance heightens our distrust in liberal democratic institutions.[33]

The spread of entertainment and surveillance technologies to all aspects of contemporary life also shapes the aesthetics of *The Wire* and other prestige TV shows. In the form of blending fact and fiction, these shows often apply highly stylized cinematography, like *The Wire*'s use of multiple camera angles and multiple modes of filming.[34] For instance, when the police pursue a criminal, objective shots from a stable camera are interspliced with subjective shots from a hand-held device. Adding to this combination of art and documentary film, we see the employment of extreme close-ups and oblique angles.[35] These aesthetic devices signal to the audience that the depicted reality is highly mediated and stylized, which adds to both the immersive and distancing effects. One of the paradoxes, then, of prestige TV is the way its gritty realism leads to total audience immersion, but the stylized aesthetics cater to ironic distance.[36]

A Fake Real War

Shows like *The Wire* want to appear realistic, but as they fictionalize reality, they undermine the modern liberal quest for truth and transparency. After all, what is supposed to define modern science and law is the impartial judgment of empirical evidence as reason functions to separate fact from fiction.[37] When this distinction between what is real and what is fiction is lost, liberal democracy is undermined. Therefore, the lost trust in science and the law is not just the result of the media exposing corrupt politicians and corrupting corporations: The culture industry itself manufactures distrust and misinformation through its aesthetic devices.[38]

We can approach this role that entertainment plays in undermining liberalism through the ways African-Americans are depicted in *The Wire*. One of the more controversial aspects of this representation is the constant use of the N-word.[39] Although it is mostly African-Americans using this term to refer to each other in a familiar way, we have to remember that it is mostly white writers putting this word into their mouths.[40] Thus, a term that has been historically used as a mode of devaluation and discrimination is employed to create a sense of realism; moreover, since it is African-Americans using it with other African-Americans, it is easily excused.[41] However, if the show is mostly watched by affluent whites, we have to ask how does the reiteration of the N-word feed into an underlying racist discourse?

In the first season, not only are the African-American characters repeating this oppressive term against themselves, but they are depicted as highly violent and sexual criminals who live in a world dominated by males and the drug trade.[42] As a mode of acceptable racism, this implicit association between African-Americans and crime helps conservative and Right-wing politicians to maintain a racist ideology, at the same time, they deny being racist.[43] In what is now called Nixon's Southern Strategy, Republicans have realized that if they want to cater to racist voters and still retain the support of people who do not want to see themselves as racist, the best solution is to use a "tough on crime" rhetoric as a substitute for direct racism.[44] In terms of the war on drugs, this political tactic has resulted in a high number of incarcerated African-American males. In fact, as Michelle Alexander argues in her *The New Jim Crow*, the systemic mistreatment of blacks in the United States has moved from slavery to segregation to incarceration.[45]

The Wire both exposes this racialized war on drugs as it also obscures its true causes and effects by turning this crucial social issue into just another source of entertainment and pleasure.[46] The white audience is then given the opportunity to "slum it" as a safe access to dangerous lifestyles is produced.[47] Within this structure, the dominant group is able to enjoy the suffering of the subordinate groups as social suffering becomes just another source for projection and entertainment. Furthermore, as I have been arguing, this production by the "liberal" media for the "liberal" audience reiterates conservative modes of racism and sexism that feeds the Right-wing backlash against minorities and the liberal welfare state.[48]

Led by a desire of the wealthy to reduce their taxes, the libertarian Right has argued that we no longer need to pay for welfare policies catering to people of color because we now live in a post-racist culture.[49] In fact, from this perspective, the only reason why we still think racism exists is because the Left invents it in order to make us feel guilty and to take our money for expensive welfare programs run by liberal politicians. Yet, at the same time, this unconscious political ideology seeks to deny the continuing presence of racism, it also relies on racism to appeal to white nationalists and white working-class people who seek to defend against their sense of lost identity and power.[50] According to this implicit logic, if downwardly mobile white workers cannot find better jobs, at least they can feel superior on a racial level.[51] While I do not think the writers of the show are intentionally trying to deny racism or re-circulate racism in a coded way, I do think that they are profiting off of the use of racist stereotypes and prejudices.[52] The gritty realism of prestige TV is then in part derived from its employment of racist and sexist cliches since the way that the dominant white audience often understands people of color is through the mediation of stereotypical representations.

Defund the Police?

At the same time that the racist fears of black-led urban crime are stoked by *The Wire*, it also depicts the police as corrupt, lazy, incompetent, bureaucratic careerists who seek to do as little policing as possible.[53] Whereas the people at the top of the police system tend to only focus on public image and political connections, many of the stars of the show are shown to heroically struggle against the system in their pursuit of the truth. What results from this structure is that the solution to these social issues is left in the hands of heroic individuals.[54]

As Christopher Lasch argues in *The Culture of Narcissism*, contemporary society is in a difficult bind because not only are so many public officials constantly lying, but the media is continuously revealing those lies (xv).[55] On the one hand, it is good to have a skeptical populace, but when everyone doubts everyone else, it becomes impossible to support liberal social institutions like the law and science.[56] This crisis in trust became very evident during the COVID-19 pandemic when the distrust of modern science, journalism, and politics resulted in a high level of preventable deaths.[57] The undermining of social trust is also demonstrated by the belief in conspiracy theories and the turn to authoritarian leaders to solve social problems.[58]

What I am arguing is that the use of racism, crime, sex, and violence for entertainment purposes has the unintended effect of destroying our faith in the very modern liberal institutions that have helped to make our lives safer, healthier, and freer.[59] Although some may say that the media is only reflecting what exists within society, we have seen how the use of fictional narratives enables the culture industry to highlight and repress particular aspects of our social existence. Meanwhile, a passive audience is given pleasure as a form of escape while serious issues become the source of entertainment.

In fact, as we watch the unfolding of the drug war, we, the audience, are also partaking in our own drug, the media.[60] Like other addictions, television relies on getting its viewers hooked and making them desire more.[61] Through the development of unsolved crimes and plot twists, the audience seeks out both stimulation and the release of tension. Here we see in an ironic, self-reflexive twist that the culture industry appears to be always reflecting on its own form and content. When we watch *The Wire*, we think we are viewing the ravages caused by a failed war on drugs, but in reality, we are lost in a fun house of mirrors as the media reflects and deflects its own addictive nature.[62]

Addiction and the Failures of the Liberal Class

It is my argument that our addiction to drugs and popular culture plays an important role in the undermining of modern liberal democratic institutions, but if we want to really understand the failures of the Democratic Party, we have to comprehend the power of the upper-middle class to transform liberal institutions from the inside. As Hedges insists, the reason why so many white working-class voters have switched to the Republican Party is that they are rightfully angry at the way the Democrats have betrayed their trust:

> These emotions spring from the failure of the liberal class over the past three decades to protect the minimal interests of the working and middle class as corporations dismantled the democratic state, decimated the manufacturing sector, looted the U.S. Treasury, waged imperial wars that can neither be afforded nor won, and gutted the basic laws that protected the interests of ordinary citizens. Yet the liberal class continues to speak in the prim and obsolete language of policies and issues. It refuses to defy the corporate assault. A virulent right wing, for this reason, captures and expresses the legitimate rage articulated by the disenfranchised. And the liberal class has become obsolete even as it clings to its positions of privilege within liberal institutions. (6)

Hedges' main point here is that as the liberal class stopped protecting the best interest of the working class, it still pretended to represent the people it was selling out.[63] This critical perspective is presented time and time again in *The Wire* as corrupt Democratic politicians are shown blocking the work of "good police."[64]

48 *The Wire* and the Death of Liberal Institutions

Meanwhile, lawyers profit from the drug war as they pursue deals that are not beneficial for society.[65]

While the second season moves to the corruption of the unions, and later seasons focus on other liberal social institutions (schools, newspapers, the Democratic party), the first season sets the tone for how a careerist mentality undermines social trust and the public good from the inside. This focus on the way people corrupt institutions from within follows Hedges' emphasis on destructive careerism. Unlike most other critiques of contemporary politics, Hedges does not privilege how social institutions are restructured by economic imperatives or social movements; instead, he reveals how bad internal incentives cater to a destructive pursuit of profit, pleasure, power, and prestige.[66] Hedges also argues that the anti-social actions of the liberal class are hidden by virtue signaling: "The liberal class, found it was more prudent to engage in empty moral posturing than confront the power elite"(9). What Hedges does not say here is how the liberal class has become the elite, and so there is no reason to expect them to go against their own self-interest.[67]

The power of Hedges analysis is evident when he shows how upper-middle-class centrists have been able to take advantage of inequality by exploiting opportunities in their own institutions:

> The liberal class refuses to recognize the obvious because it does not want to lose its comfortable and often well-paid perch. Churches and universities—in elite schools such as Princeton, professors can earn $180,000 a year—enjoy tax-exempt status as long as they refrain from overt political critiques. Labor leaders make lavish salaries and are considered junior partners within corporate capitalism as long as they do not speak in the language of class struggle. Politicians, like generals, are loyal to the demands of the corporate state in power and retire to become millionaires as lobbyists or corporate managers. Artists who use their talents to foster the myths and illusions that bombard our society live comfortably in the Hollywood Hills. (10)

One reason, then, why people distrust our liberal institutions is because centrists have traded in the public good for their own personal benefit. This form of internal corruption is portrayed throughout *The Wire* as we watch people in law enforcement lie and cheat in order to protect and enhance their careers.[68] In this competitive environment, everyone seems to only care about themselves as they misrepresent their own intentions and actions for self-protection and self-promotion.

As the drug gang member D'Angelo Barksdale states when he takes his girlfriend to a fancy restaurant: "you got money, you get to be whoever you say you are."[69] Due to the power of money and the lack of any strong countering social force, identity has been reshaped by capitalism as the only game in town. For Hedges, the undermining of the liberal class by the compulsive pursuit of profit and privilege results in an opportunity for gangsters and authoritarian politicians to take over:

> The loss of the liberal class creates a power vacuum filled by speculators, war profiteers, gangsters, and killers, often led by charismatic demagogues. It opens the door to totalitarian movements that rise to prominence by ridiculing and taunting the liberal class and the values it claims to champion. The promises of these totalitarian movements are fantastic and unrealistic, but their critiques of the liberal class are grounded in truth. (13)

It is, therefore, the self-destruction of modern liberal democratic institutions that enable anti-social leaders and criminals to gain power and control. Thus, even when the police try to do the right thing in *The Wire*, they face the resistances of a bureaucracy centered on advancing and protecting careers.[70]

At the same moment the show documents the failures of these vital liberal institutions, it is itself a product promoting the interests of its corporate sponsors. Hedges argues that the cultural industry makes liberal television writers and other commercial artists complicit by forcing them to have a role in the business of entertainment:

> The role of the liberal class in creating these sophisticated systems of manipulation has given liberals a financial stake in corporate dominance. It is from the liberal class that we get the jingles, advertising, brands, and mass-produced entertainment that keep us trapped in cultural and political illusions. And the complicity of the liberal class, cemented by the corporate salaries the members of that class earn, has sapped intellectual and moral independence. It is one of the great ironies of corporate control that the corporate state needs the abilities of intellectuals to maintain power, yet outside of this role it refuses to permit intellectuals to think or function independently. (16)

While Hedges does a good job at revealing the complicity of liberals with a destructive economic and social system, what he does not say here is that the culture industry is famous for its exploitation of labor as only a small percent of workers in the field make a sustainable wage.[71] Like the casualization of the academic labor force, "liberal" Hollywood relies on free and part-time labor as it holds out the possibility of someone winning the labor lottery.[72]

With the growing dominance of winner-takes-all industries, wealth becomes concentrated as an increasing number of workers rely on part-time gigs and multiple jobs.[73] The attraction to a life of crime is then enhanced when there appears to be little opportunity to earn an "honest living." Although shows like *The Wire* might not lead audience members to become criminals, it does function to normalize deviance as people become insensitive to violence and other anti-social behaviors.[74] As many of the criminals in the show state, it is

50 *The Wire* and the Death of Liberal Institutions

sometimes unclear what actually distinguishes crime from legal capitalism, and as we see throughout the series, these two different economic realms are often intertwined.[75] Thus, Springer Bell uses drug money to buy legitimate businesses as he plots a way to leave the drug "game." In fact, he is shown taking college business classes as he seeks to improve his social class while he learns how to effectively launder the profits from his criminal activities.[76]

Moreover, as McNulty and his associates begin to investigate Bell and the Barksdale drug gang, they discover that profits from criminal enterprises are finding their way into the hands of Democrat politicians, but they are quickly told to stop following the money.[77] The way that top brass of the police department reacts to McNulty's desire to expose the corruption of the state government relates to Hedges' argument that what ultimately undermines the liberal class and its institutions is the failure to confront the role played by capitalism as a corrosive social force:

> The liberal class was seduced by the ideology of progress—attained through technology and the amassing of national wealth, material goods, and comforts—and intimidated into supporting the capitalist destruction of reformist and radical movements. As long as the liberal class did not seriously challenge capitalism, it was permitted a place in the churches, the universities, the unions, the press, the arts, and the Democratic Party. Minimal reform, as well as an open disdain for Puritanism, was acceptable. A challenge to the sanctity of the capitalist system was not. Those who continued to attack these structures of capitalism, to engage in class warfare, were banished from the liberal cloisters. (103)

From Hedges' perspective, the liberal class was allowed to flourish as long as it did not attack capitalism in a direct way, but once Leftists started to offer a critique of the economic system, they were removed from the liberal coalition, and the Democratic Party lost its critical edge. As we see in *The Wire,* once you are no longer able to follow the money, every effort at change is undermined.

Coupled with the political and cultural refusal to counter the invasion of the market into all aspects of human life, Hedges highlights a turn to spectacle and visual knowingness:

> The media are as plagued by the same mediocrity, corporatism, and careerism as the academy, the unions, the arts, the Democratic Party, and religious institutions. The media, like the academy, hold up the false ideals of impartiality and objectivity to mask their complicity with power. They posit the absurd idea that knowledge and understanding are attainable exclusively through vision, that we should all be mere spectators of life. This pernicious reduction of the public to the role of spectators denies the media, and the public they serve, a political role.

In turning citizens into spectators, the culture industry defangs political critique as liberal institutions become complicit in promoting the values and beliefs of the dominant class. This idea of becoming merely spectators can be seen in the way that the use of wiretapping and other forms of surveillance turns the police into passive watchers of criminal activity.[78] Therefore, the very name of the series indicates the role played by technology in turning us all into passive audiences, which in a metafictional form, turns the series into a self-reflexive analysis of its own viewership.[79]

Of course, surveillance creates paranoia because no one ever knows when one is being watched or heard.[80] As we see with the spread of social media, the presenting of private lives in a public forum is commoditized as everything becomes a source and product of advertising and commercialization.[81] The culture industry, then, has been able to spread its influence into the most private aspects of people's lives, and in this form of surveillance, individuals freely expose themselves to further manipulation.[82] Moreover, the reverse side of this capitalization of the private is the way that culture takes social issues and makes them about private individuals. This move from the social to the personal mimics the "liberal" turn from a politics of social change to one of self-transformation.[83] As we shall see in the next chapter, *House of Cards* reveals what happens when the pursuit of the public good becomes subverted by a selfish form of ruthless pragmatism.

Notes

1 Sodano, Todd M. "It was TV teaching HBO's The Wire." *The Wire in the College Classroom: Pedagogical Approaches in the Humanities.* Ed. Karen Dillon. McFarland, 2015: 7–31.
2 Walters, Ben. "The Wire for tourists?." *Film Quarterly* 62.2 (2008): 64.
3 Hedges, Chris. *Death of the liberal class.* Vintage Books Canada, 2011.
4 Hedges, Chris. *Death of the liberal class.* Vintage Books Canada, 2011.
5 Caraley, Demetrios. "Washington abandons the cities." *Political Science Quarterly* 107.1 (1992): 1–30.
6 O'Brien, Benjamin Gonzalez, Loren Collingwood, and Stephen Omar El-Khatib. "The politics of refuge: sanctuary cities, crime, and undocumented immigration." *Urban Affairs Review* 55.1 (2019): 3–40.
7 Piliawsky, Monte. "The Clinton administration and African-Americans." *The Black Scholar* 24.2 (1994): 2–10.
8 Fiorina, Morris P., Samuel J. Abrams, and Jeremy C. Pope. "Culture war." *The Myth of a Polarized America* 3. Longman, 2005.
9 Kolchin, Peter. "Whiteness studies: the new history of race in America." *The Journal of American History* 89.1 (2002): 154–173.
10 Kitson, Janine. "Death of the liberal class." *Education* 94.4 (2013): 28.
11 Verene, Donald Phillip. *The art of humane education.* Cornell University Press, 2018.
12 Brown, Katherine Ann, and Todd Gitlin. "Partisans, watchdog, and entertainers." *The Oxford handbook of American public opinion and the media.* Oxford University Press, New York, 2011. 74–88.
13 Samuels, Robert. "Beyond Hillary Clinton: obsessional narcissism and the failure of the liberal class." *Psychoanalyzing the Left and Right after Donald Trump.* Palgrave Macmillan, Cham, 2016. 31–59.

14 Currinder, Marian. *Money in the house: campaign funds and congressional party politics.* Routledge, 2018.

15 Wheeler, Mark. "'A city upon a hill': The Wire and its distillation of the United States polity." *Politics* 34.3 (2014): 237–247.

16 Holt, Robin, and Mike Zundel. "Understanding management, trade, and society through fiction: lessons from The Wire." The Academy of Management Review. Vol. 39.4, 2014: 576–585.

17 Jameson, Fredric. "Realism and Utopia in 'The Wire'." *Criticism* 52.3 & 4 (2010): 359–372.

18 Dreier, Peter, and John Atlas. "The Wire–Bush–era fable about America's urban poor?." *City & Community* 8.3 (2009): 329–340.

19 Adorno, Theodor W., and Max Horkheimer. *The culture industry.* na, 2002.

20 Atlas, John, and Peter Dreier. "Is The Wire too cynical?." *Dissent* 55.3 (2008): 79–82.

21 Broersma, Marcel, and Chris Peters. "Introduction: rethinking journalism: the structural transformation of a public good." *Rethinking journalism: trust and participation in a transformed news landscape.* Routledge, 2013. 1–12.

22 Zipes, Jack. *Happily ever after: fairy tales, children, and the culture industry.* Routledge, 2013.

23 Tsudama, Laurena. "Dickensian realism in the wire." *Dickens after Dickens.* Ed. Emily Bell. White Rose University Press, 2020. 159–176.

24 Garrett, Stephen. "The rise of anti-hero." *Diunduh dari laman www. characterseven. com pada* 20 (2012).

25 Harris, Geraldine. "A return to form? Postmasculinist television drama and tragic heroes in the wake of The Sopranos." *New Review of Film and Television Studies* 10.4 (2012): 443–463.

26 Luff, Jennifer. "Featherbedding, fabricating, and the failure of authority on The Wire." *Labor: Studies in Working-Class History of the Americas* 10.1 (2013): 21–27.

27 Bonilla-Silva, Eduardo, and Austin Ashe. "The end of racism? Colorblind racism and popular media." *The Colorblind Screen: Television in Post-Racial America* 57. NYU Press, 2014.

28 Samuels, Robert. "Simon Clarke and the politics and psychoanalysis of racism." *Psychoanalysis, Culture & Society* 25.1 (2020): 96–100.

29 Haynes, Jo. "Race on The Wire: a metacritical account." *Journal for Cultural Research* 20.2 (2016): 157–170.

30 Belt, Rabia. "And then comes life: the intersection of race, poverty, and disability in HBO's The Wire." *Rutgers Race & Law Review* 13 (2011): 1.

31 Tyree, J.M. "The Wire: the complete fourth season." *Film Quarterly* 61.3 (2008): 32–38.

32 Trottier, Daniel, and David Lyon. "Key features of social media surveillance." *Internet and surveillance.* Routledge, 2013. 109–125.

33 Trottier, Daniel. *Social media as surveillance: rethinking visibility in a converging world.* Routledge, 2016.

34 Wake, Caroline. "To witness mimesis: the Politics, ethics, and aesthetics of testimonial theatre in through the wire." *Modern Drama* 56.1 (2013): 102–125.

35 Wilson, Galen. "'The bigger the lie, the more they believe': cinematic realism and the anxiety of representation in David Simon's The Wire." *South Central Review* 31.2 (2014): 59–79.

36 Watts, Robert. *Transnational television aesthetics: national culture and the "global" prestige drama.* The University of Manchester, United Kingdom, 2020.

37 Rauch, Jonathan. *The constitution of knowledge: a defense of truth.* Brookings Institution Press, 2021.

38 Tsfati, Yariv, Riva Tukachinsky, and Yoram Peri. "Exposure to news, political comedy, and entertainment talk shows: concern about security and political mistrust." *International Journal of Public Opinion Research* 21.4 (2009): 399–423.

39 Guastaferro, Wendy. "Crime, the media, and constructions of reality: using HBO'S The Wire as a frame of reference." *College Student Journal* 47.2 (2013): 264–270.

40 Lopez, Qiuana, and Mary Bucholtz. "'How my hair look?': linguistic authenticity and racialized gender and sexuality on The Wire." *Journal of Language and Sexuality* 6.1 (2017): 1–29.

41 Asim, Jabari. *The N word: who can say it, who shouldn't, and why*. HMH, 2008.

42 Brown, Keffrelyn D., and Amelia Kraehe. "Sociocultural knowledge and visual re (-) presentations of black masculinity and community: reading The Wire for critical multicultural teacher education." *The education of black males in a "post-racial" world*. Routledge, 2013. 81–98.

43 Maxwell, Angie, and Todd Shields. *The long southern strategy: how chasing white voters in the south changed American politics*. Oxford, Oxford University Press, 2019.

44 Aistrup, Joseph A. *The southern strategy revisited: republican top-down advancement in the south*. University Press of Kentucky, 2014.

45 Alexander, Michelle. "The New Jim Crow." *Power and inequality*. Routledge, 2021. 300–304.

46 Shapiro, Zachary E., Elizabeth Curran, and Rachel CK Hutchinson. "Cycles of failure: the war on family, the war on drugs, and the war on schools through HBO's The Wire." *Washington and Lee Journal of Civil Rights and Social Justice* 25 (2018): 183.

47 Thompson, Kecia Driver. "'Deserve got nothing to do with it': black urban experience and the naturalist tradition in The Wire." *Studies in American Naturalism* 7.1 (2012): 80–120.

48 Lucks, Daniel S. *Reconsidering Reagan: racism, republicans, and the road to Trump*. Beacon Press, 2020.

49 Haney-López, Ian. *Dog whistle politics: how coded racial appeals have reinvented racism and wrecked the middle class*. Oxford University Press, 2015.

50 Brown, Jessica Autumn. "The new 'southern strategy': immigration, race, and 'welfare dependency' in contemporary US Republican political discourse." *Geopolitics, History, and International Relations* 8.2 (2016): 22–41.

51 Goldstein, Donna M., and Kira Hall. "Postelection surrealism and nostalgic racism in the hands of Donald Trump." *HAU: Journal of Ethnographic Theory* 7.1 (2017): 397–406.

52 Qureshi, Bilal. "The streaming souls of White Folk." *Film Quarterly* 75.2 (2021): 80–83.

53 Penfold-Mounce, Ruth, David Beer, and Roger Burrows. "The Wire as social science-fiction?." *Sociology* 45.1 (2011): 152–167.

54 Sheehan, Helena, and Sheamus Sweeney. "The Wire and the world: narrative and metanarrative." *Jump Cut* 51 (Spring 2009): http://www.ejumpcut.org/archive/jc51.2009/Wire/index.html

55 Lasch, Christopher. *The Culture of Narcissism: American life in an age of diminishing expectations*. W. W. Norton & Company, 2018.

56 Galston, William. "Defending liberalism." *American Political Science Review* 76.3 (1982): 621–629.

57 Jaiswal, J., C. LoSchiavo, and D.C. Perlman. "Disinformation, misinformation and inequality-driven mistrust in the time of COVID-19: lessons unlearned from AIDS denialism." *AIDS and Behavior* 24.10 (2020): 2776–2780.

58 Simione, Luca, et al. "Mistrust and beliefs in conspiracy theories differently mediate the effects of psychological factors on propensity for COVID-19 vaccine." *Frontiers in Psychology* 12 (2021): 2441.

59 Pinker, Steven. *Enlightenment now: the case for reason, science, humanism, and progress*. Penguin UK, 2018.

60 Samuels, Robert. *Generation X and the rise of the entertainment subject*. Rowman & Littlefield, 2021.

61 Kubey, Robert, and Mihaly Csikszentmihalyi. "Television addiction is no mere metaphor." *Scientific American* 286.2 (2002): 74–80.

62 McIlwraith, Robert, et al. "Television addiction: theories and data behind the ubiquitous metaphor." *American Behavioral Scientist* 35.2 (1991): 104–121.

63 Abramowitz, Alan, and Ruy Teixeira. "The decline of the white working class and the rise of a mass upper-middle class." *Political Science Quarterly* 124.3 (2009): 391–422.

64 Mittell, Jason. "All in the game: The Wire, serial storytelling, and procedural logic." *Third Person: Authoring and Exploring Vast Narratives. Electronic Book Review,* (2009): 429–438.

65 Dreier, Peter, and John Atlas. "The Wire–Bush–era fable about America's urban poor?." *City & Community* 8.3 (2009): 329–340.

66 Samuels, Robert. "Beyond Hillary Clinton: obsessional narcissism and the failure of the liberal class." *Psychoanalyzing the Left and Right after Donald Trump.* Palgrave Macmillan, Cham, 2016. 31–59.

67 Nodia, Ghia. "Democracy's inevitable elites." *Journal of Democracy* 31.1 (2020): 75–87.

68 Anker, Elisabeth R. "Thwarting neoliberal security: ineptitude, the retrograde, and the uninspiring in The Wire." *American Literary History* 28.4 (2016): 759–778.

69 Read, Jason. "Stringer Bell's Lament: violence and legitimacy in contemporary capitalism." *The Wire: Urban Decay and American Television.* London: Continuim, 2009: 122–134.

70 Penfold-Mounce, Ruth, David Beer, and Roger Burrows. "The Wire as social science-fiction?." *Sociology* 45.1 (2011): 152–167.

71 Swiech, Mark R. "You'll never work in this town again: employment, economics, and unpaid internships in the entertainment and media industries." *Loyola of Los Angeles Law Review* 49 (2016): 475.

72 Miller, Toby. "The new international division of cultural labor." *Managing Media Work* Vol. 14.2 (2011): 87–99.

73 Crouch, Colin. "A long-term perspective on the gig economy." *American Affairs* 2.2 (2018): 51–64.

74 Cavender, Gray. "Normalization and deviance." *Routledge Handbook on Deviance.* Brown, Stephen E., and Ophir Sefiha, eds. Routledge, 2017: 34–44.

75 Anderson, Paul Allen. "'The game is the game': tautology and allegory in The Wire." *Criticism* 52.3 & 4 (2010): 373–398.

76 Gibson III, Ernest L. "'For whom the BELL Tolls': The Wire's stringer Bbell as tragic intellectual." *Americana: The Journal of American Popular Culture* 10.1 (2011).

77 Deylami, Shirin, and Jonathan Havercroft. *The politics of HBO's The Wire.* Taylor & Francis, 2014.

78 Wake, Caroline. "Through the (in) visible witness in through The Wire." *Research in Drama Education* 13.2 (2008): 187–192.

79 Hudelet, Ariane. "The Wire and the democracy of fiction." *Series-International Journal of TV Serial Narratives* 4.2 (2018): 77–89.

80 Giroux, Henry A. "Totalitarian paranoia in the post-Orwellian surveillance state." *Cultural Studies* 29.2 (2015): 108–140.

81 Zuboff, Shoshana. "Big other: surveillance capitalism and the prospects of an information civilization." *Journal of information technology* 30.1 (2015): 75–89.

82 McCahill, Michael, and Rachel Finn. *Surveillance, capital and resistance: theorizing the surveillance subject.* Routledge, 2014.

83 Sothern, Matthew. "You could truly be yourself if you just weren't you: sexuality, disabled body space, and the (neo) liberal politics of self-help." *Environment and Planning D: Society and Space* 25.1 (2007): 144–159.

5

HOUSE OF CARDS AND THE FALL OF THE LIBERAL CLASS

House of Cards documents the corruption of liberal institutions from within the Democratic Party.[1] As Frank Underwood seeks to gain more power at any cost, he presents a mode of ruthless pragmatism, but underlying this story of pollical manipulation is a repressed reflection on the corrosive power of the culture industry itself.[2] As one of the first shows to release an entire season at once, *House of Cards* helped to establish the aesthetic mode of binge-watching.[3] In fact, by producing a stronger, more invisible drug, the series attaches compulsive consumption to an escapist mindset as the failures of the Democratic party are documented for the viewing pleasure of a disenchanted audience.[4]

Of course, one can interpret the show through its depiction of the main protagonist, but what I want to focus on is how we can read it as a metafictional defense of the culture industry. Through the use of ironic distancing and doubling, the program makes the audience complicit in Underwood's selfish pursuit of power and pleasure, and at the same time, the use of direct address provides an ethical escape hatch for the viewers.[5] In this aesthetic structure, the "liberal" audience is told by the "liberal" writers that politics itself has become just another product of mediated mass spectacle, yet this critical message is delivered within a media production. The show then repeats what it critiques in a mode of capitalist realism and fatalism.[6] There is no outside of this system because the outside is itself produced from within the same structure.[7]

Metafiction

Throughout the first several seasons of the series, Frank Underwood punctuates the fictional narrative with direct statements made to us, the audience. While this breaking of the fourth wall should create distance between the viewers and

DOI: 10.4324/9781003352600-5

the show, the actual effect is to produce a doubled discourse where everything is both said and unsaid.[8] This doubled, ironic metafictional perspective reflects on the notion that in an age saturated by entertainment and media, all that one can do is recycle a fake reality from the perspective of knowing distance.[9] As a mode of cynical conformity, politicians who no longer believe in modern liberal democracy still have to try to compete in the game, while citizens of these democracies are socialized to conform to the system without belief in what they are doing.

Of course, the model for Underwood is Bill Clinton and his centrist, Third Way politics.[10] In *his Bobos in Paradise*, David Brooks argues that Clinton represented the blending of bohemian counter-culture and bourgeois capitalism by finding a common ground between liberals and conservatives.[11] Thus, in promoting free trade, financial deregulation, welfare reform, and the war on drugs, Clinton was able to accomplish the Republican agenda from within the Democratic Party.[12] Some see this centrist politics as an effective mode of governing, while others believe that Clinton sold out liberalism by endorsing conservative policies.[13] However, what really defines Clinton's model of governing is a cynical mode of ruthless pragmatism. According to this anti-ideology ideology, the only thing that really matters is to get elected and to stay in power.[14]

Frank Underwood, then, is a good reflection of Bill Clinton's political strategy because it is clear that the only thing Frank cares about is his own political career.[15] In fact, the first season depicts this Democrat taking on all of the most cherished Democratic policies as he seeks to rise in the ranks. Not only does Frank go against the teacher's unions and the environmentalists, but he tells the audience that "Democracy is so over-rated."[16] Frank also uses the Black Caucus in Congress to get what he wants as he lies and kills his way to a higher office.

Frank is thus an extreme representation of the negative aspects of the current Democratic Party.[17] While leaders of this party may not kill journalists or force people to commit suicide, what is accurate is the way the Democrats pretend to be the supporters of schools, unions, workers, and people of color, but their policies are mostly driven by their need to receive campaign contributions from the wealthiest top 9.9%.[18] As professional politicians catering to upper-middle-class professionals, the Democrats have abandoned the working class, but they still seek moral cover by pretending to care about these constituents.[19]

The campaign finance system, therefore, drives cynical conformity as politicians have to pretend that they are focused on one group as they seek funds from another group.[20] Within the plot of *House of Cards*, the first two seasons deal directly with this issue as the billionaire Tusk is shown to control the Democrats and the president through his secret campaign contributions.[21] In turn, Frank tries to both use Tusk's money and counter Tusk's influence at the same time. Eventually, this issue brings down the president and allows Frank the opportunity to rise to the highest position.[22]

The Media Reflection

One of the ways that Frank manipulates the system in a cynical way is through his manipulation of the journalist Zoe Barnes. Since he wants to undermine his opponents and promote his own career, he uses Zoe to leak documents in an unethical fashion.[23] It is important to point out that Zoe herself is represented as the new model of online journalism that goes against the values and processes of the older legacy media.[24] Since she is mostly driven by the desire to advance her career, she is the perfect match for Frank who seduces and uses her.[25] Once again, we see how liberal institutions are undermined by anti-social careerism. As each professional is shown to only care about his or her own advancement, the public good is sacrificed at every turn.

While some of the older journalists at the *Herald Tribune* newspaper want to protect the older liberal model of presenting the truth to advance the public good, the owner of the paper desires to turn Zoe into a star in order to help the paper compete in the new entertainment-driven model.[26] In fact, one of the ironies of the show is that it uses several real reporters as fictional characters, and here we encounter another mode of metafictional representation. Not only do we have real people playing fictional versions of themselves, but this fictional representation of real news personalities undermines our trust and belief in real journalists.[27] Since the reporting of the truth for the public good has been replaced by the culture industry's need to combine capitalist profit and entertainment, the loss of social trust in liberal institutions can be blamed in part on shows like *House of Cards*.[28] We can, thus, read this series focus on political corruption as, in part, a way of drawing attention away from how the media itself functions to corrupt society. However, through the use of ironic doubling and metafiction, these issues are both exposed and denied.

Slumming It

Coupled with his ironic asides, we experience Frank as a sociopath who sees other people as just objects to manipulate for his schemes of individual advancement.[29] For instance, he appears to have a personal bond with Freddy, the African-American owner of a barbeque restaurant he likes to visit. However, when Frank discovers that Freddy had been incarcerated, Frank drops him to protect his own self-image.[30] This relationship further highlights how some "liberal" politicians only care about people of color if it is advantageous to them. In fact, when Freddy resists selling his business, he tells the prospective buyer that white people only want to come to his place as a way of accessing his culture in a safe way: "You want them white folks to feel like they slumming … and I get to play the nigger." This notion of slumming represents the idea that people of the dominant class and race like to access the culture of poorer and darker people in order to gain a sense of authenticity or illicit pleasure.[31] Here, we find the foundations of liberal racism and the centrist fantasy of idealizing people who

58 *House of Cards* and the Fall of the Liberal Class

have been oppressed because they are seen as having a direct access to repressed, uncivilized pleasure.[32]

When *House of Cards* uses Freddy to expose the underlying racist fantasy of political centrism, this revelation has to be understood through the doubled lens of metafiction.[33] Therefore, just as Frank goes to Freddy's place to access transgressive enjoyment in a safe way, the viewers watch the series to access their own anti-social desires by living through the sociopathic behaviors of Frank Underwood.[34] Not only does this aspect of prestige TV undermine social trust in liberal institutions, but it also reveals the role centrists play in circulating racist stereotypes and prejudices.

Ultimately, the show neither endorses nor condemns Frank's anti-social undermining of modern liberal democracy.[35] Like the viewers of the series itself, *House of Cards* is divided and split; as a mode of guilty pleasure, this product of prestige TV is repulsed by what causes its attraction, and yet it still calls for an immersive, addictive mode of binge-watching.[36] In fact, the very idea of binge-watching can be related to the way streaming services, like Netflix, allow the audience the possibility of watching shows on demand.[37] Just like one can feed a baby on a schedule or by demand, TV watching caters to the unrestrained desires of the individual consumer.[38] Since one does not have to wait for a show to appear, one can watch the whole series in an addictive fashion.[39]

If we compare this development of binge-watching to the idea of feeding on schedule versus feeding on demand, we see how changes in parenting have helped to fuel the new entertainment addiction model.[40] Since from birth, people are able to demand satisfaction without delay or restraint, they become socialized to demand instant gratification without limitation.[41] This anti-social drive goes against the modern liberal notion of sacrificing in the present in order to provide for a better future. In what is often called the Protestant Work Ethic, the need to delay gratification is tied to the labor system and the development of a culture centered on controlling impulses for the common good.[42]

As we moved from an industrial economy to a consumer economy, the culture industry takes on a greater social role.[43] Since people have to be convinced to buy products they desire but may not need, the role of mass media is transformed. The new economy and culture feed off of the anti-social addictive behaviors of a populace seeking immediate satisfaction at all costs.[44] In terms of politics, the Right caters to both an unconstrained free market and the ideology of total individual freedom, while centrist seek to signal their moral virtue as they invest in competitive advantages and professional careerism.

Interestingly, Brooks argues that the Right-wing libertarians are only continuing a movement that started with 1960s counter-culture (261). According to his narrative, once the youth movement started to challenge "obsolete social norms," all standards and rules were called into question, and so the liberal consensus was undermined from the inside.[45] In other words, once the culture begins to question all authority, the lack of trust spreads to every social institution. Of course, the Right has been effective at tying both hyper-individualism and the lack of trust in liberal social institutions to a counter-revolution from above. Driven mostly by the desire of the wealthy to reduce their taxes and limit the governmental regulation of their businesses, the libertarian Right has been able to co-opt the progressive focus on individual freedom.[46] However, what *House of Cards* adds to this story is the way liberal centrists have helped to enable this coalition between the wealthy and the white working class by trading in their alliance with workers and unions for the support of upper-middle-class professionals.[47] Workers and the middle class have thus been sold out by the Democratic Party and manipulated by Republicans as the wealthiest individuals and corporations continue to run the world.

Although *House of Cards* does a good job at showing how our democratic institutions have been hollowed out from the inside, it can only reveal this issue from an ironic distance because it does not believe there is any real hope to change the system.[48] Metafictional doubling, then, serves the function of allowing for a depressing depiction of our political reality while also providing a space for distance.[49] Since we are only watching a TV show full of fictionalized representations of real people and events, we do not have to take things too seriously. Moreover, because the series is aware of its own status as a product of the culture industry, it cannot be blamed for not knowing what it is doing. Frank Underwood's cynical realism and ruthless pragmatism are the perfect match for the program's irony.[50] While the cynic competes in a system in which he no longer believes, the centrist ironist conforms to a corrupt system from the position of knowing distance. In order to comprehend politics today, it is necessary to understand this difference between the cynical Right and ironic centrists.

Bobos in Politics

As we have seen in the different prestige TV shows examined in this book, a common strategy is to present cynical, anti-social characters from an ironic, metafictional perspective. Interestingly, David Brooks, in *his Bobos in Paradise,* also uses irony and humor to examine the cultural foundations of what I have been calling centrist narcissism.[51] At the start of his book, he uses a comedic strategy to posit that what defines this new cultural order is the combination of the opposing forces of bohemian and bourgeois lifestyles:

> THIS BOOK started with a series of observations. After four and a half years abroad, I returned to the United States with fresh eyes and was confronted by a series of peculiar juxtapositions. WASPy upscale suburbs were suddenly dotted with arty coffeehouses where people drank little European coffees and listened to alternative music. Meanwhile, the bohemian downtown neighborhoods were packed with multimillion-dollar lofts and those upscale gardening stores where you can buy a faux-authentic trowel for $35.99. Suddenly massive corporations like Microsoft and the Gap were on the scene, citing Gandhi and Jack Kerouac in their advertisements. And the

60 *House of Cards* and the Fall of the Liberal Class

status rules seemed to be turned upside down. Hip lawyers were wearing those teeny tiny steel-framed glasses because now it was apparently more prestigious to look like Franz Kafka than Paul Newman. (9)

The first thing I want to highlight in this assessment of centrist narcissism is that it is focused on the contradictory combination of opposing cultural stereotypes.[52] In other words, similar to the way television shows seek to reach a diverse mass audience by portraying known, generalized features of specific groups and personality types, Brooks provides an ironic examination of cultural cliches as a form of social analysis.[53]

As a journalist who writes to get paid and recognized, Brooks is part of the culture industry, which itself is structured by the combination of art and commerce. Instead of being someone who is supposed to document the truth from an unbiased, objective viewpoint, Brooks seeks to inform and entertain at the same time.[54] Here we see how the modern liberal democratic field of journalism has been transformed by the dual need to provide pleasure and make money. Like the depiction of politics in *House of Cards*, it is vital to realize that this need to entertain frames the depictions of reality from a fictional perspective.

In fact, Brooks insists that in a previous historical era, it was possible to clearly separate art from capitalism, but in the current age, this liberal division has been lost:

> Throughout the twentieth century it's been pretty easy to distinguish between the bourgeois world of capitalism and the bohemian counterculture. The bourgeoisie were the square, practical ones. They defended tradition and middle-class morality. They worked for corporations, lived in suburbs, and went to church. Meanwhile, the bohemians were the free spirits who flouted convention. They were the artists and the intellectuals—the hippies and the Beats. In the old schema the bohemians championed the values of the radical 1960s and the bourgeois were the enterprising yuppies of the 1980s. (10)

Although one should be skeptical about Brooks' simplified, over-generalizations, this distinction between capitalism and the counter-culture does play an important role in politics, society, and subjectivity. While the Left-leaning rebels of the 1960s called for a new mode of culture, the Right-leaning urban professionals of the 1980s tended to see economic competition as the center of their lives. According to this narrative, what then happens during the age of Bill Clinton is these opposite social attitudes and political ideologies combine in an ironic, contradictory manner.[55]

Brooks posits that the new class of centrist narcissists is able to bring anti-establishment rebellion and economic conformity together:

> It was now impossible to tell an espresso-sipping artist from a cappuccino-gulping banker. And this wasn't just a matter of fashion accessories.

> I found that if you investigated people's attitudes toward sex, morality, leisure time, and work, it was getting harder and harder to separate the antiestablishment renegade from the pro-establishment company man. Most people, at least among the college-educated set, seemed to have rebel attitudes and social-climbing attitudes all scrambled together. Defying expectations and maybe logic, people seemed to have combined the countercultural sixties and the achieving eighties into one social ethos.

Even though Brooks emphasizes superficial lifestyle choices, he wants to insist that his analysis accounts for a wide range of cultural and personal attitudes. Part of this approach relies on removing subjective and political investments from his perspective so that we are presented with an anti-ideological ideology.

The primary way that Brooks is able to remove the political from politics is by tracing the cause for this ironic culture and subjectivity to the advent of a new age of information, which is itself another cultural stereotype and over-generalization:

> After a lot of further reporting and reading, it became clear that what I was observing is a cultural consequence of the information age. In this era ideas and knowledge are at least as vital to economic success as natural resources and finance capital. The intangible world of information merges with the material world of money, and new phrases that combine the two, such as "intellectual capital" and "the culture industry," come into vogue. So the people who thrive in this period are the ones who can turn ideas and emotions into products. These are highly educated folk who have one foot in the bohemian world of creativity and another foot in the bourgeois realm of ambition and worldly success. The members of the new information age elite are bourgeois bohemians. Or, to take the first two letters of each word, they are Bobos. (10)

In this description of the 9.9%, the educated elites are positioned as the ones who cash in on the use of knowledge as a form of intellectual capital.[56] Of course, the terms "culture industry" and "intellectual capital" serve the purpose of uniting together social realms that were separated during the modern liberal democratic period.[57] In other words, once science is merged with capitalism and art is combined with industry, the modern values of scientific reason and journalistic objectivity are lost. It turns out that a key aspect of liberal democracy is the social trust generated by the regulation and containment of destructive capitalistic influences. For instance, university research is supposed to be separated from financial interests so that the truth can be pursued without bias.[58] Likewise, journalists ideally base their reporting on an impartial representation of evidence.

When scholars and journalists are seen as driven by self-interest and the pursuit of profit, the public loses their trust in these important institutions. Prestige TV shows, like *House of Cards*, then produce and reflect this undermining of the liberal class from within liberalism itself. Through the use of humor, irony,

62 *House of Cards* and the Fall of the Liberal Class

metafiction, and other aesthetic devices, acclaimed programs catering to the upper-middle class flatter their audience by providing cultural knowledge as they also function to remove any sense of guilt, shame, or responsibility.[59] Ironically, Brooks admits that his own perspective and style fit this ironic form:

> Finally, a word about the tone of this book. There aren't a lot of statistics in these pages. There's not much theory. Max Weber has nothing to worry about from me. I just went out and tried to describe how people are living, using a method that might best be described as comic sociology. The idea is to get at the essence of cultural patterns, getting the flavor of the times without trying to pin it down with meticulous exactitude. Often I make fun of the social manners of my class (I sometimes think I've made a whole career out of self-loathing), but on balance I emerge as a defender of the Bobo culture. In any case, this new establishment is going to be setting the tone for a long time to come, so we might as well understand it and deal with it. (12)

Like Frank Underwood's direct addresses to the audience, Brooks' self-reflection here reveals how his own discourse must be considered to be doubled and duplicitous; he admits that he does not use a lot of statistics or classic academic methods and that his perspective combines together comedy and sociology.[60] Brooks also indicates that he is making fun of himself as he sees himself being a member of the group of which he is mocking. Like a self-reflexive, metafictional prestige TV show, this use of irony helps Brooks to escape criticism due to his awareness of the problem.[61] Moreover, he takes a fatalistic approach by claiming that we need to understand and accept this mindset because it now represents the establishment.

For Brooks, a key to the psychology of the upper-middle professional class is the desire to succeed in the capitalist game while still retaining a sense of rebellious authenticity:

> Those who want to win educated-class approval must confront the anxieties of abundance: how to show—not least to themselves—that even while climbing toward the top of the ladder they have not become all the things they still profess to hold in contempt. How to navigate the shoals between their affluence and their self-respect. How to reconcile their success with their spirituality, their elite status with their egalitarian ideals. Socially enlightened members of the educated elite tend to be disturbed by the widening gap between rich and poor and are therefore made somewhat uncomfortable by the fact that their own family income now tops $80,000. (40)

Since narcissists want to convince themselves and others that they are good people with pure intentions, they have to find a way to repress their knowledge of their complicity in an unethical system.[62] Thus, as they seek to outcompete others in an unequal society, they have to signal their virtue by claiming to be egalitarian. This narcissistic subjectivity of the 9.9% can only be explained by psychoanalysis because one has to understand that people lie to themselves to protect their own positive self-image.[63] For Freud, repression creates the unconscious and is the foundation of neurosis, and ironic centrism relies on these mechanisms of self-division.[64]

As I have been arguing, shows like *House of Cards* use irony in order to both express and repress the destructive aspects of selfish, capitalistic behavior. As a cynical opportunist, Frank Underwood presents the borderline sociopath, but his cynicism is framed in an ironic manner so that the audience can both relate to and morally condemn his behavior.[65] Since, as Freud insists, we are driven to escape feelings of guilt and shame, we need to repress our own responsibility for destructive anti-social thoughts, feelings, and actions.[66] This repression is enabled by the viewing of metafictional representations and ironic cultural analysis, which are doubled and self-divided on a formal level. As Brooks indicates, it is not just the products of the elite culture industry that are contradictory and conflicted, but the producers and consumers are also shaped by the same neurotic tendencies:

> Though they admire art and intellect, they find themselves living amidst commerce, or at least in that weird hybrid zone where creativity and commerce intersect ... This is an elite that has been raised to oppose elites. They are affluent yet opposed to materialism. They may spend their lives selling yet worry about selling out. They are by instinct antiestablishmentarian yet somehow sense they have become a new establishment. (41)

This combination of conflicting ideological investments results in a mode of subjectivity reliant on repression and the symptomatic combination of opposite traits.[67] The new elites do not want to be seen as elites because they seek to hide their selfish pursuits of pleasure, profit, privilege, and prestige behind the moral virtues of equality and anti-materialism.

Like the Democratic party itself, these members of the upper-middle class have to veil their anti-social exploitation of inequality in order to maintain a positive self-image:

> The members of this class are divided against themselves, and one is struck by how much of their time is spent earnestly wrestling with the conflict between their reality and their ideals. They grapple with the trade-offs between equality and privilege ("I believe in public schooling, but the private school just seems better for my kids"), between convenience and social responsibility ("These disposable diapers are an incredible waste of resources, but they are so easy"), between rebellion and convention ("I know I did plenty of drugs in high school, but I tell my kids to Just Say No"). (41)

64 *House of Cards* and the Fall of the Liberal Class

While Brooks argues that these centrists are constantly thinking about their conflicting investments and beliefs, our understanding of obsessional narcissism tells us that most of these conflicts are repressed and projected onto cultural fantasies or expressed through unconscious symptoms, dreams, and anxiety.[68] In fact, anxious feelings often result because the true content of a conflict is repressed into the unconscious.[69]

Instead of exploring the contradictory nature of the narcissistic centrists in a clear and straightforward way, Brooks turns to humor to reconcile the differences shaping this mode of politics and subjectivity: "The grand achievement of the educated elites in the 1990s was to create a way of living that lets you be an affluent success and at the same time a free-spirit rebel. Founding design firms, they find a way to be an artist and still qualify for stock options" (42). This comic reflection on the conflict between wealth and social justice helps Brooks to smooth over the edges of an important social and psychological division:

> Building gourmet companies like Ben & Jerry's or Nantucket Nectars, they've found a way to be dippy hippies and multinational corporate fat cats. Using William S. Burroughs in ads for Nike sneakers and incorporating Rolling Stones anthems into their marketing campaigns, they've reconciled the antiestablishment style with the corporate imperative. Listening to management gurus who tell them to thrive on chaos and unleash their creative potential, they've reconciled the spirit of the imagination with service to the bottom line. (42)

Brooks uses humor here to reconcile capitalism and art, but we have to comprehend how irony allows one to say one thing and also to take back what one is saying.[70] This rhetorical strategy helps people to protect the innocence of their own self as they mock the world around them.[71] However, the ironic use of comedy can also place the self itself into question.

Humor, irony, and metafiction may look like they are able to reconcile social and psychological conflicts, but these imaginary combinations rely on repression and self-division. For instance, the following passage hides the destructive effects of inequality and the concentration of wealth in contemporary society:

> Turning university towns like Princeton and Palo Alto into entrepreneurial centers, they have reconciled the highbrow with the high tax bracket. Dressing like Bill Gates in worn chinos on his way to a stockholders' meeting, they've reconciled undergraduate fashion with upper-crust occupations. Going on eco-adventure vacations, they've reconciled aristocratic thrill-seeking with social concern. Shopping at Benetton or the Body Shop, they've brought together consciousness-raising and cost control. When you are amidst the educated upscalers, you can never be sure if you're living in a world of hippies or stockbrokers. In reality you have entered the hybrid world in which everybody is a little of both. (92)

House of Cards and the Fall of the Liberal Class **65**

These efforts to combine consumerism with social activism can represent a cover for destructive, anti-social actions. Furthermore, the application of the market to everything from university research to ecological concern undermines the modern liberal separation of capitalism from science and democracy.[72] What then helps to threaten our trust in essential social institutions is our awareness that people are using money to corrupt systems for their own self-interest. After all, this is the message we get in *House of Cards* and many other prestige TV shows: Nothing and no one can be trusted because everyone and everything is shaped by market value and the pursuit of personal profit.[73]

In the final chapter of his book, Brooks directly addresses contemporary politics and Bill Clinton's centrist, Third Way strategy:

> The politicians who succeed in this new era have blended the bohemian 1960s and the bourgeois 1980s and reconciled the bourgeois and bohemian value systems. These politicians do not engage in the old culture war rhetoric. They are not podium-pounding "conviction politicians" of the sort that thrived during the age of confrontation. Instead, they weave together different approaches. They triangulate. They reconcile. They know they have to appeal to diverse groups. They seek a Third Way beyond the old categories of left and right. They march under reconciling banners such as compassionate conservatism, practical idealism, sustainable development, smart growth, prosperity with a purpose. (256)

This celebration of the compromising combination of liberalism and conservativism functions to idealize moderates as the symptomatic coalescing of opposites. However, as *House of Cards* reveals, there might be a dark side behind Bill Clinton's strategy. After all, Frank Underwood does not turn to Republican policies because he thinks they are good and effective; instead, everything he does is based on his desire to increase and maintain his power.[74] In fact, when you have two opposed ideological distortions, bringing them together and finding a middle ground does not mean that one has determined an effective policy or politics. Furthermore, Brooks' own analysis tends to see this combination of opposites as an ironic escape from conflict and responsibility.

After using comedy to laugh at the upper-middle class' efforts to hide selfish individualism behind a veil of progressive rhetoric, Brooks' turns around and praises Bill Clinton for basing his policies on an ideal middle-ground:

> Whatever its other features, the Clinton/Gore administration embodied the spirit of compromise that is at the heart of the Bobo enterprise. In the first place, the Clintons were both 1960s antiwar protesters and 1980s futures traders. They came to the White House well stocked with bohemian ideals and bourgeois ambitions. They campaigned against the "tired old labels of left and right." In 1997 Bill Clinton effectively summarized his policy approach in a speech to the Democratic Leadership Council: "We

had to go area by area to abandon those old false choices, the sterile debate about whether you would take the liberal or conservative positions, that only succeeded in dividing America and holding us back."

This speech by Clinton is echoed in the third season of *House of Cards* when Frank announces that he is going to scale back welfare policies in order to pass his jobs bill.[75] Rather than seeing this strategy as a middle-ground compromise, we should interpret both Frank's and Clinton's use of Republican policies as a way to gain power and control. This mode of centrist politics is centered on hiding an anti-social agenda behind a progressive discourse, and as we saw throughout the Clinton administration, this Democrat was better than most Republican presidents at getting a Republican agenda signed into law.

For a moderate like Brooks, Clinton's centrist pragmatism should be recognized for its ability to overcome all cultural and political conflict by finding a compromised middle ground:

> Confronted with a culture war that pitted traditional values against liberationist values, the Clinton administration merged, blurred, and reconciled. The Clintonites chose three key words—"Opportunity, Responsibility, and Community"—as their perpetual campaign themes, rarely pausing over whether there might be tensions between them. They embraced school uniforms and other traditional-sounding gestures, as well as condoms in schools and other liberal-sounding measures. Clinton triangulated above the hard-edged warriors on left and right and presented a soft and comfortable synthesis. He could, he declared, balance the budget without painful budget cuts, reform welfare without meanness, mend affirmative action but not end it, toughen the drug war while spending more on rehabilitation, preserve public schools while championing charter school alternatives. Battered early in the administration with a culture war skirmish over gays in the military, the Clintonites settled on "Don't Ask, Don't Tell." If ever there was a slogan that captures the Third Way efforts to find a peaceful middle ground, that was it.

Of course, the whole strategy of the "Don't Ask, Don't Tell" policy rests on the use of repression and censorship in order to hide from others the truth, and this employment of lies sits at the center of the Clinton's centrist strategies.[76] As Freud argues, neurotic symptoms function by bringing together opposites in a contradictory structure where tension and anxiety are replaced by a fantasized resolution.[77] In the case of Clinton's policy for gays in the military, the goal was to allow for homosexuality and its moral rejection at the same time.[78] From one angle, one can argue that this is an effective policy, but from another angle, it functions to keep hate and discrimination alive by hiding it from view.

Brooks believed when he published this book in 2000 that Clinton's Third Way strategy was being exported around the world, and soon a new era of peace and reconciliation would reign:

> This Third Way approach, neither neatly liberal nor conservative, neither a crusading counterculturalist nor a staid bourgeois, is a perpetual balancing act. And now if you look across the industrialized world, you see Third Way triangulators perched atop government after government. A few decades ago theorists predicted that members of the New Class would be more ideological than previous classes, more likely to be moved by Utopian visions and abstract concepts. In fact, when the children of the 1960s achieved power, they produced a style of governance that was centrist, muddled, and if anything, anti-ideological. (257–258)

By claiming that centrism is a politics beyond ideology, Brooks' idealized a strategy that simply repressed real conflicts as it smuggled anti-social policies under the banner of keeping peace and making progress. Of course, right after Brooks wrote this book, 9/111 occurred, and the whole rhetoric of the end of ideology and conflict disappeared.

Brooks' idealization of centrist compromise should be read as an upper-middle-class rationalization of upper-middle-class values and beliefs. As the ideology of the top 9.9%, the main effect is to idealize the concentration of wealth and power in an age of growing inequality. In fact, Brooks does, at times, recognize how centrists represent the ruling ideas of the ruling class:

> They have settled on this style of politics because this is what appeals to the affluent suburbanites and to the sorts of people who control the money, media, and culture in American society today. Today there are about nine million households with incomes over $100,000, the most vocal and active portion of the population. And this new establishment, which exerts its hegemony over both major American political parties, has moved to soften ideological edges and damp down doctrinal fervor. Bobo Democrats sometimes work for investment houses like Lazard Frères. Bobo Republicans sometimes listen to the Grateful Dead. They don't want profound culture-war-type confrontations over first principles or polarizing presidential campaigns. (258)

It should not be too surprising that the people who are profiting the most from the system want to keep it going: It also should not be news that one way that these centrists have been able to keep their control over the Democratic Party is by undermining Left-leaning politicians like Bernie Sanders.[79] Just as Frank Underwood does not hesitate to screw over everyone on his Left, centrist Democrats protect their interests by appropriating and defanging Left-wing

68 *House of Cards* and the Fall of the Liberal Class

policies. By turning issues of class conflict into battles over racism and sexism, these moderates have been able to signal their virtue as they continue to enhance their power and profit.[80]

It is important to realize that what is being called the center and middle ground is actually the top 9.9% of the wealth bracket, and so it is wrong to think of this group as representing the shared interests of all Americans. By seeing the rich and powerful as the moderate compromise, most of the middle class is removed from the picture:

> Whereas the old Protestant Establishment was largely conservative Republican, the new Bobo establishment tends to be centrist and independent. In 1998 the National Journal studied the voting patterns of America's 261 richest towns and discovered that they are moving to the center. The Democratic vote in those communities has risen in every election over the past two decades as members of the educated class have flooded into tony places like Wayne, Pennsylvania. The Democrats won 25 percent of the rich vote in 1980 and 41 percent in 1996. In that year Bill Clinton carried 13 of the 17 most affluent congressional districts. (258–259)

This reliance of the Democratic Party on the support and votes of the educated wealthy means that it no longer really represents the working class or most of the middle class. It is then little wonder why so many white workers without college degrees have migrated to the Republican party.[81] Furthermore, as I have been arguing throughout this book, prestige TV caters to this demographic, and so it is important to see why white, educated, urban elites are so attracted to this type of entertainment.

Not only have Democrats, like the fictional Frank Underwood and the real Bill Clinton, alienated their former constituents by passing legislation that caters to the upper-middle class, but the Democratic establishment has sought to eliminate the influence that the Left has in its own party. For Brooks, this shift represents a positive change:

> The affluent suburbs send moderate Republicans or moderate Democrats to Capitol Hill. These politicians spend much of their time in Congress complaining about the radicalism of their colleagues from less affluent districts. They can't understand why their liberal and conservative brethren seem addicted to strife. The less affluent polarizers rant and rave on Crossfire. They are perpetually coming up with radical and loopy ideas—destroy the IRS, nationalize health care. They seem to feel best about themselves when they are alienating others. All of this is foreign to the politicians from the Range Rover and Lexus districts. Like their Bobo constituents, they are more interested in consensus than conquest, civility than strife. (259)

Brooks' biased perspective caters to the people he is mocking with his comedic sociology, but the joke is really on the people who expect their elected liberal officials to act like real liberals. In turn, his elite audiences can laugh knowingly at his humorous analysis as they remain safe in their upscale homes. While Brooks' labels universal healthcare as a loopy and radical idea, millions of Americans go into poverty to pay for a system that does not exist in other "developed" nations.[82]

What is really ironic is that at the very moment Brooks was singing his praise of the moderates, these centrists were being replaced in the Republican Party by the extreme Right.[83] One possible reason why Brooks is so wrong in his analysis and predictions is that he fundamentally does not understand the foundations of the libertarian Right. For example, in the following passage, he equates individual freedom with the values of both the bohemian liberals and the conservative bourgeoisie:

> The bohemian sixties and the bourgeois eighties were polar opposites in many ways. But they did share two fundamental values: individualism and freedom. Writers in both decades paid lip service to community action and neighborhood institutions, but the main effort was to liberate individuals. The bohemian revolt in the sixties was about cultural freedom. It was about free expression, freedom of thought, sexual freedom. It was an effort to throw off social strictures and conformist attitudes, to escape from the stultifying effects of large bureaucracies and overbearing authority figures. The bourgeois resurgence of the 1980s, on the other hand, expanded economic and political freedom. The economy was deregulated and privatized in order to unleash entrepreneurial energies. The nanny state was attacked and in some cases rolled back. (260)

What Brooks misses in this historical analysis is the way that many bohemians were anti-capitalist, and the Right has often appropriated aspects of the counter-culture, like the push for free speech, in order to promote a free market approach.[84]

Instead of focusing on how the wealthy have tried to game the system by reducing taxes and governmental regulation, Brooks focuses on the ways the counter-cultural Left undermined important social institutions:

> If you start dissolving social ties in order to unleash individual self-expression, pretty soon you'll notice that valuable community bonds are eroded as well. Efforts to weaken oppressive authority end up corroding all authority. The stature of teachers, parents, and democratic institutions gets diluted along with that of bureaucratic despots and uptight busybodies ... If the sixties and the eighties were about expanding freedom and individualism, the Bobos are now left to cope with excessive freedom and excessive individualism. (261)

70 *House of Cards* and the Fall of the Liberal Class

On one level, Brooks is correct to highlight how cultural authority and liberal democratic institutions have been undermined by the focus on individuals over social constraints, but on another level, what he misses is how the culture industry has played a major role in tying rebellion to capitalism.[85] By selling products and entertainment as a mode of freedom and escape from social control, the anti-capitalist aspects of the counter-culture have been absorbed into the market. Brooks' idealized combination of the bohemian and the bourgeois, thus, really represents the dominance of capitalism in all aspects of culture. While Frank Underwood says that he prefers power over money, he also realizes that he needs money to gain power.[86] Likewise, the producers of prestige TV shows like to highlight how much they spend on creating their elite shows, which cater to a mostly upper-middle-class audience.[87] From the perspective of the culture industry, it is important to follow the money and give the wealthy what the wealthy want, and this often entails male anti-heroes manipulating others for their own personal advantage.

As I have been arguing, this dark vision of contemporary life feeds the upper-middle class' desire to survive in an unequal and dangerous world through the pursuit of self-interest regardless of how it affects others. Frank Underwood, then, is a perfect symbol for this type of pathology that underlies the narcissism of the 9.9%. As we shall see in the next chapter by looking at *Dexter,* the culture industry not only provides the perfect drug to help us escape our social reality, but it also circulates an ideology that furthers our social distrust. By representing a serial killer as a likable law enforcement officer, we encounter yet another example of prestige TV's investment in an anti-social, anti-hero.

Notes

1 Delledonne, Giacomo. "House of cards: comparing the British and the American TV series from a constitutional perspective." *Polemos* 12.1 (2018): 107–122.
2 Davidson, Lindsey E. "The world according to Frank underwood: politics and power in 'House of Cards'." Senior Thesis. (2015): https://scholarship.claremont.edu/cmc_theses/1052
3 Jenner, Mareike. "Is this TVIV? On Netflix, TVIII and binge-watching." *New Media & Society* 18.2 (2016): 257–273.
4 Pittman, Matthew, and Kim Sheehan. "Sprinting a media marathon: uses and gratifications of binge-watching television through Netflix." *First Monday* 20 (10), 2015.
5 Sorlin, Sandrine. "Breaking the fourth wall." *The Pragmatics of Personal Pronouns* 171 (2015): 125.
6 Birke, Dorothee, and Robyn Warhol. "Multimodal you: playing with direct address in contemporary narrative television." *How to Do Things with Narrative: Cognitive and Diachronic Perspectives* (2017): 141–55.
7 Liu, Alan. "The power of formalism: the new historicism." *ELH* 56.4 (1989): 721–771.
8 Schlütz, Daniela M., Daniel Possler, and Lucas Golombek. "'Is he talking to me?': how breaking the fourth wall influences enjoyment." *Projections* 14.2 (2020): 1–25.
9 Aken, Niki. "What's the meta?." *Storyline* 33 (2013): 72–76.
10 Matchett, Stephen. "Political power and the white house—'the west wing, boss, Lincoln, House of Cards'." *Sydney Institute Quarterly, The* 42 (2013): 10–17.

House of Cards and the Fall of the Liberal Class **71**

11 Brooks, David. *Bobos in paradise: the new upper class and how they got there.* Simon and Schuster, 2010.
12 Giddens, Anthony. *The Third Way and its critics.* John Wiley & Sons, 2013.
13 Jones, Daniel Stedman. "The neoliberal origins of the Third Way: how Chicago, Virginia and Bloomington shaped Clinton and Blair." *The SAGE Handbook of Neoliberalism* (2018): 167.
14 Feffer, John. "The Human Rights Agenda." *New Politics* 10.2 (2005): 162.
15 Sorlin, Sandrine. "Strategies of involvement and moral detachment in House of Cards." *Journal of Literary Semantics* 47.1 (2018): 21–41.
16 Hackett, J. Edward. *House of Cards and philosophy: Underwood's republic.* John Wiley & Sons, 2015.
17 Shea, Brendan. "House of Cards as philosophy: democracy on trial." *The Palgrave Handbook of Popular Culture as Philosophy*, Springer, 2020: 1–22.
18 Ferguson, Thomas. *Golden rule: the investment theory of party competition and the logic of money-driven political systems.* University of Chicago Press, 1995.
19 Stonecash, Jeffrey M., et al. "Class and party: secular realignment and the survival of democrats outside the south." *Political Research Quarterly* 53.4 (2000): 731–752.
20 Primo, David M. "Public opinion and campaign finance: reformers versus reality." *The Independent Review* 7.2 (2002): 207–219.
21 Keller, James R. "The vice in vice president: House of Cards and the morality tradition." *Journal of Popular Film and Television* 43.3 (2015): 111–120.
22 Meyer, Matt. "Why Underwood is frankly not an overman." *House of Cards and Philosophy: Underwood's Republic.* Springer, 2015: 68–80.
23 Kajtár, László. "Rooting for the villain: Frank Underwood and the lack of imaginative resistance." *House of Cards and Philosophy: Underwood's Republic.* Springer 2015: 227–236.
24 Kantola, Anu. "Liquid journalism." In *The Sage Handbook of Digital Journalism.* Sage, 2016: 424–442.
25 McNair, Brian. "From cinema to TV: still the same old stories about journalism." *Jourlism Practice* 8.2 (2014): 242–244.
26 Ferrucci, Patrick, and Chad Painter. "Print versus digital: how medium matters on House of Cards." *Journal of Communication Inquiry* 41.2 (2017): 124–139.
27 Ferrucci, Patrick. "Mo 'meta' blues: how popular culture can act as metajournalistic discourse." *International Journal of Communication* 12 (2018): 18.
28 Manoliu, Ioana Alexandra. "Like and dislike. Negativity bias in political TV series." *Commposite* 19.3 (2017): 5–22.
29 Pilipets, Elena, and Rainer Winter. "House of Cards—House of Power: political narratives and the cult of serial sociopaths in narrative politics in American quality dramas in the digital age." *Politics and politicians in contemporary US Television.* Routledge, 2016. 113–126.
30 Gonzalez-Sobrino, Bianca, Emma González-Lesser, and Matthew W. Hughey. "On-demand diversity? The meanings of racial diversity in Netflix Productions." *Challenging the status quo.* Brill, 2018. 321–344.
31 Berruz, Stephanie Rivera. "The spice of white life." (2016). https://www.academia.edu/19018611/The_Spice_of_White_Life_Freddy_and_Racist_Representations
32 Samuels, Robert. "Simon Clarke and the politics and psychoanalysis of racism." *Psychoanalysis, Culture & Society* 25.1 (2020): 96–100.
33 Mackay, Ruth. "Reflexive modes and narrative production: metatextual discourse in contemporary American narrative." *Canadian Review of American Studies* 44.1 (2014): 65–84.
34 Piccinin, Fabiana, and Gabriel Steindorff. "O Narratário Como Confidente: Metaficção E Quebra Da Quarta Parede Em 'House Of Cards'." *Linguagens-Revista de Letras, Artes e Comunicação* 11.1 (2017): 148–160.
35 Hackett, J. Edward. *House of Cards and philosophy: Underwood's republic.* John Wiley & Sons, 2015.

36 Pittman, Matthew, and Kim Sheehan. "Sprinting a media marathon: uses and gratifications of binge-watching television through Netflix." *First Monday* (2015). https://doi.org/10.5210/fm.v20i10.6138

37 Matrix, Sidneyeve. "The Netflix effect: teens, binge watching, and on-demand digital media trends." *Jeunesse: Young People, Texts, Cultures* 6.1 (2014): 119–138.

38 Jenner, Mareike. "Is this TVIV? On Netflix, TVIII and binge-watching." *New Media & Society* 18.2 (2016): 257–273.

39 KULAK, Önder. "The binge-watching experience on Netflix." *Yedi* 24 (2020): 45–55.

40 Law, Clarice S. "The impact of changing parenting styles on the advancement of pediatric oral health." *Journal of the California Dental Association* 35.3 (2007): 192–197.

41 Hubbs-Tait, Laura, et al. "Parental feeding practices predict authoritative, authoritarian, and permissive parenting styles." *Journal of the American Dietetic Association* 108.7 (2008): 1154–1161.

42 Furnham, Adrian. "The Protestant work ethic: a review of the psychological literature." *European Journal of Social Psychology* 14.1 (1984): 87–104.

43 Rifkin, Jeremy. *The age of access: the new culture of hypercapitalism.* Penguin, 2001.

44 Wilk, Richard. "Poverty and excess in binge economies." *Economic Anthropology* 1.1 (2014): 66–79.

45 Carter, April. *Direct action and liberal democracy.* Routledge, 2013.

46 Frank, Thomas. *One market under God: extreme capitalism, market populism, and the end of economic democracy.* Anchor Canada, 2001.

47 Frank, Thomas. *Listen, liberal: or, what ever happened to the party of the people?.* Macmillan, 2016.

48 Manoliu, Ioana Alexandra. "Watching House of Cards: connecting perceived realism and cynicism." *Atlantic Journal of Communication* 27.5 (2019): 324–338.

49 Currie, Mark. *Metafiction.* Routledge, 2014.

50 Jones, Patrick, and Gretchen Soderlund. "The conspiratorial mode in American television: politics, public relations, and journalism in House of Cards and Scandal." *American Quarterly* 69.4 (2017): 833–856.

51 Drew, Rob. "'Once more, with irony': karaoke and social class." *Leisure Studies* 24.4 (2005): 371–383.

52 Armstrong, Paul B. "The politics of irony in reading Conrad." *Conradiana* 26.2/3 (1994): 85–101.

53 Verdaguer, Pierre. "A turn-of-the-century honeymoon?." *French Politics, Culture & Society* 21.2 (2003): 50–63.

54 Kim, Eunjoon, and Morgan Sheng. "The postsynaptic density." *Current Biology* 19.17 (2009): R723–R724.

55 Pollin, Robert. "The Anatomy of Clintonomics." *New Left Review 3: 14-46.*

56 Florida, Richard. "Cities and the creative class." *City & Community* 2.1 (2003): 3–19.

57 Throsby, David. "Cultural capital." *Journal of Cultural Economics* 23.1 (1999): 3–12.

58 Washburn, Jennifer. *University, Inc.: the corporate corruption of higher education.* Basic Books, 2008.

59 Samuels, Robert. "The pleasure principle and the death drive." *Freud for the twenty-first century.* Palgrave Pivot, Cham, 2019. 17–25.

60 Metcalf, Roy. "Lo, the Poor WASP." *Social Policy* 31.2 (2000): 55–55.

61 Hutcheon, Linda. "The complex functions of irony." *Revista canadiense de estudios hispánicos.* 16.2 (Winter 1992): 219–234.

62 Dovi, Suzanne. "'Making the world safe for hypocrisy'?." *Polity* 34.1 (2001): 3–30.

63 Freud, Sigmund. "Notes upon a case of obsessional neurosis." *The Standard Edition of the complete psychological works of Sigmund Freud, Volume X (1909): two case histories ("Little Hans" and the "Rat Man").* Simon and Schuster. 1955. 151–318.

64 Freud, Sigmund. "Repression." *The Standard Edition of the complete psychological works of Sigmund Freud, Volume XIV (1914–1916): on the history of the psycho-analytic movement, papers on metapsychology and other works.* 1957. 141–158.

65 Klarer, Mario. "Putting television 'aside': novel narration in House of Cards." *New Review of Film and Television Studies* 12.2 (2014): 203–220.

66 Samuels, Robert. "Transference and Narcissism." *Freud for the twenty-first century.* Palgrave Pivot, Cham, 2019. 43–51.

67 Samuels, Bob. "Neoliberalism and higher ed." *Psychoanalysis, Culture & Society* 19.1 (2014): 47–51.

68 Samuels, Robert. "Beyond Hillary Clinton: obsessional narcissism and the failure of the liberal class." *Psychoanalyzing the Left and Right after Donald Trump.* Palgrave Macmillan, Cham, 2016. 31–59.

69 Freud, Sigmund. *The uncanny.* Penguin, 2003.

70 Stewart, Jon. *Søren Kierkegaard: subjectivity, irony, & the crisis of modernity.* Oxford University Press, 2015.

71 Magill, R. Jay. *Chic ironic bitterness.* University of Michigan Press, 2009.

72 Frank, Thomas, and Matt Weiland, eds. *Commodify your dissent: salvos from the baffler.* W. W. Norton & Company, 1997.

73 Smith, Geoff, and Rahul Telang. "House of Cards." (2016): 3–15.

74 Pilipets, Elena, and Rainer Winter. "House of Cards—House of Power: political narratives and the cult of serial sociopaths in narrative politics in American quality dramas in the digital age." *Politics and politicians in contemporary US Television.* Routledge, 2016. 113–126.

75 Davidson, Lindsey E. "The world according to Frank Underwood: politics and power in 'House of Cards'." Sebior Thesis (2015). http://scholarship.claremont.edu/cmc_theses/1052

76 Borch III, Fred L. "The history of don't ask, don't tell in the army: how we got to it and why it is what it is." *Military Law Review* 203 (2010): 189.

77 Freud, Sigmund. "Hysterical phantasies and their relation to bisexuality." *The Standard Edition of the complete psychological works of Sigmund Freud, Volume IX (1906–1908): Jensen's "Gradiva" and Other Works.* Simon and Schuster. 1959. 155–166.

78 Kramer, Michael. "Don't settle for hypocrisy." *Time* 142.4 (1993): 41–41.

79 Hedges, Chris. *Death of the liberal class.* Vintage Books Canada, 2011.

80 Frank, Thomas. *Listen, liberal: or, what ever happened to the party of the people?.* Macmillan, 2016.

81 Manza, Jeff, and Ned Crowley. "Working class hero? Interrogating the social bases of the rise of Donald Trump." *The Forum* 15.1. (2017: 3–28.

82 Schwartz, Stephan A. "American healthcare: a profile in shortages." *Explore: The Journal of Science and Healing* 12.3 (2016): 167–170.

83 Kabaservice, Geoffrey. *Rule and ruin: the downfall of moderation and the destruction of the Republican Party, from Eisenhower to the Tea Party.* Oxford University Press, 2012.

84 Samuels, Robert. "Catharsis: the politics of enjoyment." *Zizek and the rhetorical unconscious.* Palgrave Macmillan, Cham, 2020. 7–31.

85 Frank, Thomas, and Matt Weiland, eds. *Commodify your dissent: salvos from the baffler.* W. W. Norton & Company, 1997.

86 Byron, Chris, and Nathan Wood. "'Money gives power … well, a run for its money': Marx's observations on why capital and not Frank is really in charge of the White House." *House of Cards and philosophy: Underwood's republic. Springer,* 2015: 152–162.

87 Gonzales, Julia. "His dark materials: did you watch the first episode?." *UWIRE Text* (2019): 1–1.

6

DEXTER

Artistic Violence as Class Distinction

Many prestige shows, like *Dexter*, focus on the theme of vigilante justice.[1] Part of this fascination with people who step outside of the law to impose their own law or retribution is derived from the combination of a lost faith in modern liberal social institutions coupled with the promotion of a libertarian investment in hyper-individualism.[2] It is also no accident that these avenging angels are usually white males who have decided to take the law into their own hands.[3] In the case of *Dexter*, we learn that his adoptive father tried to control his son's psychopathic tendencies by creating a code of conduct. Here the father's law is seen as supplementing the social law since Dexter is trained to only kill people who deserve to be killed, and most of these deserving victims are ones that the official criminal justice system has failed to catch or imprison.[4]

Of course, it is no easy feat to get an audience to empathize with a serial killer, but the show enlists many different strategies to make us root for him and feel his pain—even if he may not be able to feel our pain.[5] On the most basic level, Dexter is represented as a good person who loves his sister and is good at his job as a blood expert for the Miami police. His psychopathology is also partially excused by his early trauma of seeing his mother murdered.[6] However, what really allows us to both relate and not relate to his actions is the use of several aesthetic distancing techniques. Not only is Dexter constantly narrating his own thoughts for the audience, but the show relies on the use of artistic camera angles and saturated colors to remind us that we are watching art and not a direct depiction of reality.[7] Moreover, art itself functions here as a method of class distinction, which enables the upper-middle class to signal its elite status.[8]

DOI: 10.4324/9781003352600-6

Artist as Serial Killer

As someone who examines blood at crime scenes, Dexter mixes science and art while he presents an aestheticized representation of violent acts.[9] Furthermore, his voice-overs tell the audience that he is always aware of what he is doing, and thus even his most heinous acts are done from the position of expert knowledge.[10] The audience, then, is pushed to identify with his expertise as we become seduced into a complicit relationship. As our desire for knowledge is heightened by the show's constant use of mysteries and cliffhangers, we gain pleasure by identifying with Dexter's secret knowledge.[11]

It is, therefore, easy to forget that Dexter is a serial killer who must constantly lie to keep his secret life hidden. In fact, one thing that many of the prestige TV shows have in common is that their main characters are often lying to everyone around them.[12] This continuous representation of deceit must have some effect on the audience since even if we are let in on the truth, we know that everyone else is believing in untruths. In a society where everyone lies, it is no wonder why so many people have lost trust in our modern liberal institutions: If we are constantly exposed to deceitful people, we have no reason to believe that politicians, the police, scientists, or journalists can be trusted.[13] Once again, we have to ask if these prestige shows are only documenting what is happening in society or are they helping to cause the social issues they depict?

In terms of *Dexter*, are the police unable to catch and imprison criminals like Dexter and his victims because no system is perfect, or has a culture of careerism undermined this liberal democratic institution? It appears that we want too much and ask too little of the systems that are supposed to protect us and allow for us to live healthy, productive lives. We also do not trust these systems because all the media usually shows us is when they fail.[14] Not only does the news emphasize crime and corruption, but fictional television shows also tend to attract an audience by depicting the worst aspects of human behavior and social institutions.[15] From the perspective of the Left, pervasive sexism and racism undermine the criminal justice system, while conservatives tend to believe we are too soft on criminals and crime.[16] For liberal centrists, virtue signaling often results in a weak call for reform, yet as I have documented throughout this book, the same people who want to be seen as pursuing justice and fairness are often the ones who are only concentrating on their own careers and individual survival.

In the case of *Dexter,* it appears that the failures of the "liberal" Miami police system require people like the main character to take matters into their own hands.[17] Instead of having to play politics like everyone else at the station, Dexter can act as his own judge and jury. While he is at times stymied and blocked by the official justice system, these frustrations only motivate him to pursue justice on his own terms.[18] And yet, we should not forget that he is also represented as a psychopathic killer with little empathy or emotion. In fact, one of the themes of

76 *Dexter*

the series is that Dexter has to train himself how to fake human emotions so that others will not detect his true nature.[19]

Our Dark Passenger

It is also vital to note that his constant references to his murderous impulses as his "dark passenger" function to separate his violent tendencies from the rest of his personality.[20] It is as if his id has been split off into a different being that has been fully shaped by trauma, and this splitting helps the audience to care about him and not reject his character for his evil actions.[21] We can always say that it isn't really Dexter who is committing these horrible acts—it's just the dark passenger who rides along with him. However, we still have to ask why does this prestige TV show go to such lengths to get us to care about a serial killer?

On one level, we can say that we all feel frustrated by the social system, and so we identify with the impulse to take matters into our own hands, but do we really want to extend our empathy and identification to such a monster?[22] Why do we find it enjoyable and interesting to view such depraved acts? Yes, we always can say that we are just watching a show about a fictional character performing fictional acts; however, we still need to account for the popularity of such a series. From a psychoanalytic perspective, we all have a dark side or dark passenger, and so we desire to see these actions and impulses acted out by others.[23] One can even argue that popular culture serves as an important safety valve for our violent tendencies, and therefore, one reason why we have become less murderous over time as a species is that we have replaced committing acts of violence with watching fictionalized others perform these transgressions.[24] Yet, from the perspective of political ideology, we should examine the desire to see acts of vigilante justice from within the structure of a modern liberal democracy. In other terms, what political group benefits from these depictions?

For conservatives invested in maintaining social stability and the social hierarchy, the representation of crime helps to stigmatize devalued groups as it fortifies calls for strong leaders and enhanced morality.[25] In response to this ideology, the Left tends to see the criminal justice system as racist and unjust, and so depictions of the failure of the social order support their call to eliminate or at least radically change the current legal institutions.[26] Responding in part to this Leftist revolt, Right-wing politicians seek to take justice in their own hands as they focus on individual rights and freedom.[27] The Right is then able to bond with conservatives over a shared effort to equate crime with race. Meanwhile, the liberal center seeks out a slow reform of the justice system to appease the Left and realize the central values of modern liberal democracy, but moderates, like Bill Clinton, also have a tendency to appease conservatives by criminalizing people of color.[28] Ironically, Clinton's effort to pursue the drug war and fight urban crime was coupled with his effort to be seen as a champion of the African-American community.[29]

What conservatives, centrists, Leftists, and Right-wingers all fail to realize is that the modern liberal legal system, where the law is king instead of the king being the law, is centered on the establishment of necessary but impossible ideals like impartiality, equality, and fair treatment.[30] As a work-in-progress, democratic justice will never be perfect or completely just, but its failures can only be viewed against its ideals. Moreover, democratic law must be impersonal and impartial, and so it is not centered on individualism.[31] In fact, when people take the law into their own hands, they undermine the system and spread social distrust. Since modern liberal institutions rely on social belief combined with empirical testing, they avoid both the dangers of conservative blind faith and the libertarian ideology of unregulated individual liberty.

The main way that a show like *Dexter*, then, undermines liberal democracy is by combining the failures of the official justice system with the heroic efforts of the isolated individual to make things right. For example, in the first season, Dexter kills a man who is polluting the Internet with extreme videos of him killing people. When Dexter takes care of this criminal by eliminating him, he is also gesturing to the way that the media, in general, needs to be cleaned up through individual acts of vigilante justice and not the promotion of better, more effective laws.[32]

Murder as Art

The first season also depicts a serial killer who treats his victims as art projects as he displays their dismembered body parts in what can only be called public art instillations.[33] In bringing together art and murder, the show both aestheticizes crime as it shows the connection between art and death.[34] On the most basic level, art freezes life and replaces living entities with dead representations.[35] At the same time, when crime and violence are treated as art, they enter into an unclear moral space. However, from a metafictional perspective, the series' equivalence of art and murder points to the unconscious acknowledgment that the culture industry itself feeds off of the glorification of violence.[36] It is not just that Dexter turns crime scenes into art through his use of red thread and other visual techniques; the program itself seeks to make crime a source for viewing pleasure.[37]

Although there is an ongoing debate concerning how the depiction of violence affects audiences, one thing we know for sure is that people who watch a lot of news and crime shows tend to see the world as more dangerous than it actually is.[38] This heightened sense of crime and threat calls for authoritarian responses as people retreat into the safety of their homes only to watch more representations of criminality. Part of the result of this process is a lost trust in modern social institutions coupled with an increased willingness to use conspiracy theories to make sense of the world.[39] In fact, there is sometimes little difference between the techniques of detectives and the interpretive strategies of conspiracy

78 *Dexter*

theorists: In both cases, one seeks to find an underlying order by connecting together seemingly detached clues.[40]

Police shows then tend to increase our social paranoia as we learn to fill the gaps in our knowledge through the use of delusional pattern recognition.[41] While it is at times difficult to distinguish between scientific investigation and psychotic delusion, what determines the difference is what Freud called the humility of our perspective.[42] Instead of believing that we have all the answers and everything is connected, we have to understand how modern science works through approximation and consensus. This view of the limits of knowledge is in direct contrast to the role of scientism that we often find in neuroscience and evolutionary psychology.[43] In fact, what we witness in *Dexter* and other contemporary police procedurals is a reliance on genetics as the true source of evidence.[44] Not only do genetic traces help to resolve crimes, but criminal behavior is seen as driven by biological inheritance.

Even though we are told that Dexter's pathology is derived from an early trauma, we are also shown that he is not in control of his own impulses, and therefore he is driven by his genes and his biology.[45] Since he cannot stop his dark passenger, he is a helpless victim of an internalized foreign element. From this perspective, nothing is really his fault since his genes or his trauma have made him turn to a life of crime. Furthermore, these impulses have been rationalized and directed by his adoptive father, who wants him to use his anti-social drives for good.[46]

From one perspective, we can read the way that Dexter's anti-social impulses are mediated by his adoptive father's code as indicating the combination of libertarian ideology and conservative patriarchy. As a way of explaining the strange coalition between religious conservatives and free market libertarians, we are shown how the perverse rejection of the social law can be united with an insistence on masculine order and conservative hierarchy.[47] In revealing the perverse underside of the traditional order, we understand how conservative ideology has always relied on an underlying anti-social violence.[48]

Of course, this deep understanding of the Republican coalition is not directly stated by the series. After all, fictional shows are supposed to show and not tell, and thus the underlying meaning has to be revealed through conscious interpretation, which itself can be compared to a conspiracy theory. However, what I have been arguing for is a mode of analysis that seeks to eliminate the biases of the Left, the Right, conservatives, and centrists by exposing how these ideologues function to undermine social trust and our investment in modern liberal democracy.

The Role of Art in Centrist Ideology

Ultimately, *Dexter* forces us to confront the issue of how art has reshaped reality as everything, including serial killers, becomes an object of aesthetic representation and cathartic pleasure. According to Jean Baudrillard's *Conspiracy of Art*, we have now entered a cultural period where art and artifice have been so successful in spreading their influence that life itself appears as an image or simulation (26).[49] For instance, with *Dexter*, the use of saturated colors, strange camera angles, and soundtrack create a situation where the viewer is constantly reminded that they are watching a stylized, artificial fiction, and yet, the power of the show comes from its realism and the way it gets the audience to empathize with the main character.[50] In other words, like so many other prestige TV shows, *Dexter* relies on representing reality and fiction at the same time, and in this way, it makes the fake world seem real and the real world appear fake.

As a mode of ironic doubling, the combination of realism and hyper-stylized artistic expression places the audience in a divided, contradictory position, where everything is both serious and unserious as the voyeuristic access to violence is both affirmed and denied. For Baudrillard, this doubling effect results in subjective indifference since it is no longer possible to clearly separate fact from fiction.[51] When everything becomes a spectacle and a commodity, we lose the space for critical distance or an unbiased perspective.[52] The fundamental institutions of liberal democracy and science are then challenged by a world where it is no longer possible to separate capitalism, art, and politics.

In fact, in his *Audience of One*, James Poniewozik refers to Aldous Huxley's *Brave New World* and Neil Postman's *Amusing Ourselves to Death* in order to argue that the artistic replacement of reality with images has been the dominant effect of television:[53]

> In Huxley's dystopia, the people were controlled not by force and propaganda but by pleasure—games, drugs, and phenomenally immersive entertainments. "Orwell thought we would be marched single-file and manacled into oblivion," Postman said. "Huxley thought we would dance ourselves there, with an idiot smile on our face." For Postman, the pied piper was TV; it elevated the image over the word and thus appearance over substance. (xiv)

Postman's argument, then, matches Baudrillard's claim that our sense of reality has been undermined by the dominance of art, artifice, and images.[54] From this perspective, not only does Dexter turn crime scenes into art projects, but the show itself replaces life and death with mostly visual aesthetics.

For Poniewozik, this dominance of image over substance and reality not only defines television but also politicians like Donald Trump:

> Donald Trump made himself out of television. He treated his life as a show. He knew that it was better to seem like New York's most successful businessman than to actually be it. The seeming was something you could leverage and license and sell. He understood that if you presented the right picture within the four corners of a camera frame—glitter, competence,

80 *Dexter*

> überstrength—it didn't matter that the backdrop was Sheetrock or that just outside the shot was a bare soundstage and floodlights. (xix)

The argument here is that Trump's presidency was made possible by the dominance of the televisual object. From this perspective, Trump is not even really a person since he is more like an image or a character that is presented on a television show.[55] As politics and life itself become so mixed with art and artifice, we can no longer separate fact from fiction or good from evil.[56] In fact, by producing both a gritty realism and an artistic distance at the same time, prestige TV shows like *Dexter* cater to the divided subjectivity of centrist narcissists who have to find a way to deny their own anti-social desires. This ironic mode of politics and subjectivity is, therefore, in contrast with the cynical ruthless pragmatism of someone like Trump.

What we find in *Dexter* is another ironic framing of a cynical subject: So the issue is not that art and life have completely merged; rather, an anti-social model of libertarian pleasure and immersion is being viewed from the lens of ironic contradiction. Since the centrist, narcissistic upper-middle class wants to repress their own feelings of shame and guilt related to their exploitation of an unequal society, they have to project their desire onto cultural fantasies and then deny the meaning and value of what they are seeing.

The Art of the 9.9%

To further understand the culture and the subjectivity of the narcissistic, centrist upper-middle class, we can look at Pierre Bourdieu's *Distinction: A Social Critique of the Judgement of Taste*.[57] According to this sociological perspective, art appreciation is based on education and upbringing and not on natural impulses: "Whereas the ideology of charisma regards taste in legitimate culture as a gift of nature, scientific observation shows that cultural needs are the product of upbringing and education: surveys establish that all cultural practices (museum visits, concert-going, reading etc.), and preferences in literature, painting or music, are closely linked to educational level (measured by qualifications or length of schooling) and secondarily to social origin" (1). For Bourdieu, one is not born appreciating certain types of art; rather, one learns what to like, and this education is determined by class.

Just as cable TV corporations had to find a way to differentiate their product from standard television by producing and reinforcing the values of prestige consumption, elite art relies on a host of social institutions that transform class into taste: "To the socially recognized hierarchy of the arts, and within each of them, of genres, schools or periods, corresponds a social hierarchy of the consumers. This predisposes tastes to function as markers of 'class'" (1). Not only can you often determine someone's political affiliation based on what products they consume, but their class position determines what they think about art.[58]

While Dexter turns crime scenes into art, the creators of the series transform television into high culture in order to attract an upper-middle-class audience.[59] The very idea of prestige TV, then, functions as a class distinction, as the educated, meritocratic elite seek to distinguish their precious tastes from the low culture of the masses: "Culture also has its titles of nobility—awarded by the educational system—and its pedigrees, measured by seniority in admission to the nobility" (2). This notion of nobility is displaced in a meritocratic system as educational attainment often becomes a proxy for class level.[60] Moreover, people in elite educational institutions are not only provided with a coveted and scarce social value, but they are also socialized to appreciate and devalue certain modes of culture.

As Bourdieu insists, this educating of taste begins at an early age and is developed both inside and outside of school: "Even in the classroom, the dominant definition of the legitimate way of appropriating culture and works of art favours those who have had early access to legitimate culture, in a cultured household … " (2). This process of legitimating different forms of art in order to signal class is essential to the way cable corporations relied on elevating their own productions by debasing network television.[61] In this process of class distinction, prestige TV is associated with masculine high art, while network television is equated with feminized mass consumption.[62]

It is thus not a natural thing to call cable programs prestigious since this term of valuation requires the social construction of taste and appreciation based on class distinctions:

> A work of art has meaning and interest only for someone who possesses the cultural competence, that is, the code, into which it is encoded. The conscious or unconscious implementation of explicit or implicit schemes of perception and appreciation which constitutes pictorial or musical culture is the hidden condition for recognizing the styles characteristic of a period, a school or an author, and, more generally, for the familiarity with the internal logic of works that aesthetic enjoyment presupposes. (2)

The appreciation of art then requires the learning of specific codes, which can be conscious or unconscious. Interestingly, *Dexter* has its main character constantly telling the audience how he has to learn how to conform to social expectations because he is a psychopath with little emotion.[63] In other words, Dexter has to learn the social codes that shape taste and expected norms for his class, race, and gender.

For Bourdieu, a key move is to reveal how our taste and appreciation for art is based on the learning of cultural codes that are often determined by social position: "Thus the encounter with a work of art is not 'love at first sight' as is generally supposed, and the act of empathy, *Einfühlung*, which is the art-lover's pleasure, presupposes an act of cognition, a decoding operation, which implies the implementation of a cognitive acquirement, a cultural code" (3). Like Dexter, we have to learn these codes because we are not born with them. Through our families, peers, and education, we internalized what Freud called the ideals of

82 *Dexter*

the ego, and it is from these ideals that we not only judge others but judge ourselves.[64]

Just as narcissists crave the recognition of others in order to define themselves as good and valuable, the upper-middle class uses the ideology of meritocracy and prestige to determine value.[65] Bourdieu adds that this process of socialization occurs on an unconscious level, as taste is seen as being natural, spontaneous, and personal:

> This typically intellectualist theory of artistic perception directly contradicts the experience of the art-lovers closest to the legitimate definition; acquisition of legitimate culture by insensible familiarization within the family circle tends to favour an enchanted experience of culture which implies forgetting the acquisition. The 'eye' is a product of history reproduced by education. This is true of the mode of artistic perception now accepted as legitimate, that is, the aesthetic disposition, the capacity to consider in and for themselves, as form rather than function, not only the works designated for such apprehension, i.e., legitimate works of art, but everything in the world, including cultural objects ... (3)

The way we see not only art but ourselves and the world around us, therefore, relies on internalizing cultural codes and then acting as if these codes do not exist. From this perspective, we do not see reality; instead, we perceive everything through the filter of education and socialization.[66]

What ultimately defines elite art for Bourdieu is the valuing of form over content, and this means that prestige is derived from a separation from economic and social necessity: "An art which, like all Post-Impressionist painting, is the product of an artistic intention which asserts the primacy of the mode of representation over the object of representation demands categorically an attention to form which previous art only demanded conditionally" (3). The artist, then, triumphs over the world by replacing practical needs with a concern for the formal elements of the artwork: "The pure intention of the artist is that of a producer who aims to be autonomous, that is, entirely the master of his product, who tends to reject not only the 'programmes' imposed a priori by scholars and scribes, but also—following the old hierarchy of doing and saying—the interpretations superimposed a posteriori on his work" (3). The artist gains power and autonomy by using formal elements to go beyond reality and necessity. In this structure, the content does not really matter because what is important is the ability of the artist to transcend the referent of the representation: "To assert the autonomy of production is to give primacy to that of which the artist is master, i.e., form, manner, style, rather than the 'subject', the external referent, which involves subordination to functions even if only the most elementary one, that of representing, signifying, saying something" (3). Although Bourdieu focuses on the way art appreciation is based on education and culture, he also wants to position the artist as a free imposer of form over content.

This power of the artist to transcend content is ultimately derived from the freedom from economic necessity, and therefore it has a class basis:

> It also means a refusal to recognize any necessity other than that inscribed in the specific tradition of the artistic discipline in question: the shift from an art which imitates nature to an art which imitates art, deriving from its own history the exclusive source of its experiments and even of its breaks with tradition. An art which ever increasingly contains reference to its own history demands to be perceived historically; it asks to be referred not to an external referent, the represented or designated 'reality', but to the universe of past and present works of art. (4)

Art for art's sake is thus derived from the leisure class' freedom from economic necessity and practical reality.[67] It is, therefore, mostly the wealthy who have the time and resources to truly appreciate great art as they signal their prestige through their conspicuous consumption of unneeded products. Watching prestige TV shows, then, may signal that one has the resources and free time to indulge in form over content.[68] Likewise, prestige TV shows indicate their association to high art by using camera angles, colors, and sounds that are not centered on developing the plot or character.

Furthermore, when people talk about the prestige TV shows they are watching, they are signaling to others their ability to enjoy artistic form in opposition to the lower modes of cultural consumption. People who have the time and money to binge-watch elite shows are able to enjoy a mode of television that is pretentious and class-based: "This is seen clearly in the case of the novel and especially the theatre, where the working-class audience refuses any sort of formal experimentation and all the effects which, by introducing a distance from the accepted conventions (as regards scenery, plot, etc.), tend to distance the spectator, preventing him from getting involved and fully identifying with the characters" (4). Immersive culture, like reality TV and computer games, allows for a total identification between the viewer and the viewed, but this type of "working-class" culture resists any formal experimentation that creates distance between the object and the subject.

This opposition between artistic culture and working-class culture helps to explain why upper-middle-class centrists tend to prefer prestige TV over common network programs and why the "uneducated" white working-class members of the Republican Party often prefer sports, game shows, soap operas, network comedies, and reality programs.[69] However, it is vital to see how race, gender, and class feed into these distinctions. Moreover, it is not just that certain groups of people who like certain types of television vote in a certain way, but the way that people view television is dependent in part on their political ideology and personal psychopathology.

Prestige TV shows like *Dexter*, therefore, cater to a particular class, and this recruitment of a specific audience necessitates a certain level of formal

84 *Dexter*

experimentation: "In contrast to the detachment and disinterestedness which aesthetic theory regards as the only way of recognizing the work of art for what it is, i.e., autonomous, *selbständig*, the 'popular aesthetic' ignores or refuses the refusal of 'facile' involvement and 'vulgar' enjoyment, a refusal which is the basis of the taste for formal experiment" (4). Selective cable shows can be more artistic because they do not have to cater to a mass audience; however, this conception of art relies on producing and generating class differences.[70]

Fromm a classist position, art for art's sake requires a mode of freedom from necessity that only comes from having a certain level of power and resources:

> Whereas, in order to grasp the specificity of the aesthetic judgement, Kant strove to distinguish that which pleases from that which gratifies and, more generally, to distinguish disinterestedness, the sole guarantor of the specifically aesthetic quality of contemplation, from the interest of reason which defines the Good, working-class people expect every image to explicitly perform a function, if only that of a sign, and their judgements make reference, often explicitly, to the norms of morality or agreeableness. Whether rejecting or praising, their appreciation always has an ethical basis. (5)

Bourdieu argues here that working-class audiences want every image in a TV show to perform a clear function, while the upper-class elites have the freedom and time to appreciate art that serves no direct function. Prestige TV can be said to be gratuitous because excess is allowed to people who have the time and money to waste.

Bourdieu's analysis is not only about class but itself tends to replicate the very class system he is critiquing. For instance, he labels non-elite audiences as naïve and prosaic:

> The very seriousness (or naivety) which this taste invests in fictions and representations demonstrates a contrario that pure taste performs a suspension of 'naive' involvement which is one dimension of a 'quasi-ludic' relationship with the necessities of the world ... Intellectuals could be said to believe in the representation—literature, theatre, painting—more than in the things represented, whereas the people chiefly expect representations and the conventions which govern them to allow them to believe 'naively' in the things represented. (5)

In this simple binary, elite intellectuals are seen as being interested in art and representation, while the masses have a naïve and realism-based approach to culture and the world. This classist analysis can be critiqued, but it also does effectively reveal how prestige TV has differentiated itself from network television.

By catering to the upper-middle class members who have the time and resources to pay for expensive cable subscriptions, prestige TV can increase its profits and raise its reputation; however, as Bourdieu insists, this appeal to elite values rests on an amoral distance from social reality and economic necessity:

> The pure aesthetic is rooted in an ethic, or rather, an ethos of elective distance from the necessities of the natural and social world, which may take the form of moral agnosticism (visible when ethical transgression becomes an artistic *parti pris*) or of an aestheticism which presents the aesthetic disposition as a universally valid principle and takes the bourgeois denial of the social world to its limit. The detachment of the pure gaze cannot be dissociated from a general disposition towards the world which is the paradoxical product of conditioning by negative economic necessities—a life of ease—that tends to induce an active distance from necessity. (6)

Aesthetic distance is therefore tied to an upper-middle-class life of ease and disposable income for the leisure class.[71] For instance, as Dexter turns crime scenes into art and Showtime separates itself from lower-class products, the production of taste remains anchored to inequality and class hierarchy:

> In fact, through the economic and social conditions which they presuppose, the different ways of relating to realities and fictions, of believing in fictions and the realities they simulate, with more or less distance and detachment, are very closely linked to the different possible positions in social space and, consequently, bound up with the systems of dispositions (habitus) characteristic of the different classes and class fractions. Taste classifies, and it classifies the classifier. (6)

Bourdieu's great contribution here is to clearly tie aesthetic taste to class as he examines how class distinctions are produced and maintained. Prestige TV is, then, one of the ways that elites signal to each other their elite status as they show off their ability to indulge in amoral activities lacking a functional purpose.

This drive to produce prestigious culture for elites often functions by taking popular forms of mass culture and repurposing them for a refined audience. For instance, we shall see in the next chapter how *Game of Thrones* effectively transforms the low-brow genre of Medieval fantasy fiction into an expression of high art. While many viewers of this series are attracted to its uncensored depictions of sex, violence, and profanity, what really helps to turn this show into high art is the way that it projects current conceptions of gender and race onto a fictionalized past. On the most fundamental level, *Game of Thrones* traces the movement from an initial Medieval conservative ideology to a postmodern Left-wing feminine revenge of the oppressed. Yet, this revolution is ultimately put down at the end of the series through the reversal of the minority-based rebellion. While this counter-revolution does appear to cater to a Right-wing backlash politics, the metafictional framing absorbs this cultural fantasy into the centrist, upper-middle-class unconscious realm of guilty pleasures.

86 *Dexter*

Notes

1 Ford, Jessica, and Amy Boyle. "The emotional detective: gender, violence and the post-forensic TV crime drama." (2021).

2 McConachie, Bruce. "Neoliberal politics, polarized films, and authoritarianism, 2000–2020." *Drama, Politics, and Evolution*. Palgrave Macmillan, Cham, 2021. 227–285.

3 Alsop, Elizabeth. "Sorority flow: the rhetoric of sisterhood in post-network television." *Feminist Media Studies* 19.7 (2019): 1026–1042.

4 Smith, Victoria L. "Our serial killers, our superheroes, and ourselves: showtime's Dexter." *Quarterly Review of Film and Video* 28.5 (2011): 390–400.

5 Hartmann, Matthew. *Wound culture and genre: a study on vigilante justice in "Dexter".* Diss. Hawaii Pacific University, 2012.

6 Gibbs, Alan. "'You make yourself into a monster so you no longer bear responsibility for what you do': Dexter, naturalism, and neoliberal crime discourse." *Studies in American Naturalism* 15.2 (2020): 211–235.

7 Granelli, Steven, and Jason Zenor. "Decoding 'The Code': reception theory and moral judgment of Dexter." *International Journal of Communication* 10 (2016): 23.

8 Murdock, Graham. "Pierre Bourdieu, distinction: a social critique of the judgement of taste." *International Journal of Cultural Policy* 16.1 (2010): 63–65.

9 Sienkiewicz-Charlish, Agnieszka. "A Serial killer with a heart: crime and morality in Dexter Agnieszka Sienkiewicz-Charlish." *Fatal Fascinations: Cultural Manifestations of Crime and Violence* (2014): 121.

10 Brylla, Catalin. "Why do we love Dexter Morgan in the morning?." *The Art of the Title Sequence* (2010).

11 Houwen, Janna. "Identifying with Dexter." *American, British and Canadian Studies* 24 (2015): 24–43.

12 Mittell, Jason. *Complex tv.* New York University Press, 2015.

13 Falcone, Rino, and Cristiano Castelfranchi. "Social trust: a cognitive approach." *Trust and deception in virtual societies.* Springer, Dordrecht, 2001. 55–90.

14 Cappella, Joseph N., and Kathleen Hall Jamieson. "News frames, political cynicism, and media cynicism." *The Annals of the American Academy of Political and Social Science* 546.1 (1996): 71–84.

15 Sodano, Todd M. "It was TV teaching HBO's The Wire." In *The Wire in the College Classroom: Pedagogical Approaches in the Humanities.* McFarland, 2015: 7.

16 Roberts, Julian V., and Loretta J. Stalans. *Public opinion, crime, and criminal justice.* Routledge, 2018.

17 NURSE, ANGUS. "Decoding the dark passenger: the serial killer as a force for justice. Adapting Jeff Lindsay's Dexter for the small screen." *Law and Justice on the Small Screen.* Oxford, 2012: 403–424.

18 Olivier, Bert. "When the 'Law' no longer suffices: Dexter." *South African Journal of Art History* 27.3 (2012): 52–67.

19 DePaulo, Bella. *The psychology of Dexter.* BenBella Books, Inc., 2010.

20 Nurse, Angus. "Decoding the dark passenger: the serial killer as a force for justice. Adapting Jeff Lindsay's Dexter for the small screen." *Law and Justice on the Small Screen* (2012).

21 MacDonald, Alzena. "Dissecting the 'dark passenger': reading representations of the serial killer." In *Murders and Acquisitions: Representations of the Serial Killer in Popular Culture.* New York: Bloomsbury, 2013: 1–13.

22 Granelli, Steven, and Jason Zenor. "Decoding 'The Code': reception theory and moral judgment of Dexter." *International Journal of Communication* 10 (2016): 23.

23 Mosse, Hilde L. "Aggression and violence in fantasy and fact." *American Journal of Psychotherapy* 50.4 (1996): 421–426.

24 Pinker, Steven. *The better angels of our nature: why violence has declined.* Penguin Books, 2012.

25 Newell, Walker. "The legacy of Nixon, Reagan, and Horton: how the tough on crime movement enabled a new regime of race-influenced employment discrimination." *Berkeley Journal of African-American Law & Policy* 15 (2013): 3.

26 Alexander, Michelle. "The New Jim Crow." *Power and inequality.* Routledge, 2021. 300–304.

27 Sundar, Nandini. "Vigilantism, culpability and moral dilemmas." *Critique of Anthropology* 30.1 (2010): 113–121.

28 Takei, Carl. "From mass incarceration to mass control, and back again: how bipartisan criminal justice reform may lead to a for-profit nightmare." *University of Pennsylvania Journal of Law & Social Change* 20 (2017): 125.

29 Piliawsky, Monte. "The Clinton administration and African-Americans." *The Black Scholar* 24.2 (1994): 2–10.

30 Kolm, Serge-Christophe. *Modern theories of justice.* MIT Press, 2002.

31 Greif, Avner. "History lessons: the birth of impersonal exchange: the community responsibility system and impartial justice." *Journal of economic perspectives* 20.2 (2006): 221–236.

32 Smith, Victoria L. "Our serial killers, our superheroes, and ourselves: showtime's Dexter." *Quarterly Review of Film and Video* 28.5 (2011): 390–400.

33 Tyree, Joshua M. "Spatter pattern." *Film Quarterly* 62.1 (2008): 82–85.

34 Peeters, Carla. "The beauty is in the eye of the beheader. the aesthetics of murder in the talented Mr Ripley, the silence of the lambs and darkly dreaming Dexter." Dissertation: https://matheo.uliege.be/handle/2268.2/12461

35 Baudrillard, Jean. *Symbolic exchange and death.* Sage, 2016.

36 Izzo, Donatella. "A hall of mirrors: the sublime object of justice in Dexter." *Ex-Centric Narratives: Journal of Anglophone Literature, Culture and Media* 1.1 (2017): 105–121.

37 Green, Stephanie. "Desiring Dexter: the pangs and pleasures of serial killer body technique." *Continuum* 26.4 (2012): 579–588.

38 Jöckel, Sven, and Hannah Früh. "'The world ain't all sunshine': investigating the relationship between mean world beliefs, conservatism and crime TV exposure." Journal of Communications (2016) 41(2): 195–217.

39 Jamieson, Patrick E., and Daniel Romer. "Violence in popular US prime time TV dramas and the cultivation of fear: a time series analysis." *Media and Communication* 2.2 (2014): 31.

40 Moore, Alfred. "Conspiracies, conspiracy theories and democracy." *Political Studies Review* 16.1 (2018): 2–12.

41 Boltanski, Luc. *Mysteries and conspiracies: detective stories, spy novels and the making of modern societies.* John Wiley & Sons, 2014.

42 Freud, Sigmund. "Totem and taboo: some points of agreement between the mental lives of savages and neurotics (1913 [1912–13])." *The Standard Edition of the complete psychological works of Sigmund Freud, Volume XIII (1913–1914): totem and taboo and other works.* 1955. VII–162.

43 Lessl, Thomas M. "Naturalizing science: two episodes in the evolution of a rhetoric of scientism." *Western Journal of Communication (includes Communication Reports)* 60.4 (1996): 379–396.

44 Bull, Sofia. "Hunting minds, hunting genes: from profiling to forensics in TV serial killer narratives." In *Murders and Acquisitions: Representations of the Serial Killer in Popular Culture.* Bloomsbury, 2013: 203.

45 Berryessa, Colleen, and Taylor Goodspeed. "The brain of Dexter Morgan: the science of psychopathy in Showtime's season 8 of Dexter." *American Journal of Criminal Justice* 44.6 (2019): 962–978.

46 Force, William Ryan. "The code of Harry: performing normativity in Dexter." *Crime, Media, Culture* 6.3 (2010): 329–345.

47 Gregoriou, Christiana. "'Times like these, I wish there was a real Dexter': unpacking serial murder ideologies and metaphors from TV's Dexter internet forum." *Language and Literature* 21.3 (2012): 274–285.

88 *Dexter*

48 Žižek, Slavoj. *The plague of fantasies.* Verso, 1997.

49 Kellner, Douglas. "Baudrillard and the art conspiracy." *Jean Baudrillard.* Routledge, 2008. 107–120.

50 Brylla, Catalin. "Why do we love Dexter Morgan in the morning?." *The Art of the Title Sequence* (2010): https://www.artofthetitle.com/assets/WhydoweloveDexter-MorganintheMorningbyCatalinBrylla.pdf?k=4c213bc993

51 Sandywell, Barry. "Forget Baudrillard?." *Theory, Culture & Society* 12.4 (1995): 125–152.

52 Jameson, Frederic. "Excerpts from postmodernism, or the cultural logic of late capitalism." *A Postmodern Reader* (1993): 312–332.

53 Poniewozik, James. *Audience of one: Donald Trump, television, and the fracturing of America.* Liveright Publishing, 2019.

54 Postman, Neil. *Amusing ourselves to death: public discourse in the age of show business.* Penguin, 2005.

55 Ouellette, Laurie. "The Trump show." *Television & New Media* 17.7 (2016): 647–650.

56 Baudrillard, Jean. *The transparency of evil: essays on extreme phenomena.* Verso, 1993.

57 Bourdieu, Pierre. *Distinction a social critique of the judgement of taste.* Routledge, 2018.

58 Grenfell, Michael, and Cheryl Hardy. *Art rules: Pierre Bourdieu and the visual arts.* Berg, 2007.

59 Tokgöz, Yigit. "The rise of the anti-hero: pushing network boundaries in the contemporary US television." *Kadir Has Üniversitesi* Masters Thesis (2016): https://www.academia.edu/28815501/The_Rise_of_The_Anti_Hero_Pushing_Network_Boundaries_in_The_Contemporary_U_S_Television

60 Rivera, Lauren A. *Pedigree.* Princeton University Press, 2016.

61 Newman, Michael Z., and Elana Levine. *Legitimating television: media convergence and cultural status.* Routledge, 2012.

62 Nygaard, Taylor, and Jorie Lagerwey. "Broadcasting quality: re-centering feminist discourse with The Good Wife." *Television & New Media* 18.2 (2017): 105–113.

63 Pisters, Patricia. "Dexter's plastic brain: mentalizing and mirroring in cinematic empathy." *Dexter's Plastic Brain: Mentalizing and Mirroring in Cinematic Empathy. Film and Media Studies Journal, 14* (2014): 53–63.

64 Milrod, David. "The ego ideal." *The Psychoanalytic Study of the Child* 45.1 (1990): 43–60.

65 Yair, Gad. "Meritocracy." *The Blackwell Encyclopedia of Sociology. Wiley,* 2007.

66 Nisbett, Richard E., and Yuri Miyamoto. "The influence of culture: holistic versus analytic perception." *Trends in Cognitive Sciences* 9.10 (2005): 467–473.

67 Singer, Irving. "The aesthetics of 'art for art's sake'." *The Journal of Aesthetics and Art Criticism* 12.3 (1954): 343–359.

68 Kendall, Diana Elizabeth. *The power of good deeds: privileged women and the social reproduction of the upper class.* Rowman & Littlefield, 2002.

69 Fioroni, Sarah Bachleda, et al. "Political sorting in US entertainment media." *Popular Communication* vol. 20.2 (2021): 1–16.

70 Newman, Michael Z., and Elana Levine. *Legitimating television: media convergence and cultural status.* Routledge, 2012.

71 Veblen, Thorstein, and C. Wright Mills. *The theory of the leisure class.* Routledge, 2017.

7

GAME OF THRONES

Climate Change, Gender Wars, and the Fictionalized Past

Game of Thrones performs the difficult task of making the past come alive. Set in a fictional Medieval period, the series allows for a seamless combination of truth and fiction and the past and the present.[1] In fact, it is the argument of this chapter that the show is shaped by projecting a contemporary gender war into the past as the premodern patriarchal order becomes threaten by the rise of female characters who are then ultimately contained and controlled as a crippled male is made king at the end.[2] Known for its realism and unconstrained sex, violence, and profanity, the show presents the fantasy of a static gender hierarchy upset by the enhanced power of women, minorities, and people with disabilities.[3]

One lingering question is whether the rise of the oppressed is a representation of a revolutionary, Leftist politics or does this rebellion only exist so it can be put down in the form of a reactionary backlash? Moreover, it is not only oppressed minorities who seek power and revenge but supranatural beings and the dead themselves rise from the ashes and threaten the dominant order.[4] As a return to the primitive primary processes, the animistic breakdown between what is alive and what is dead places the entire narrative within the realm of a cultural fantasy.[5] In fact, according to Freud, this level of "primitive" thought revolves around the confusion between our own thoughts and the perception of the external world.[6] Yet, it would be wrong to say that the show is just one long psychotic projection or dream; instead, we need to see how the historical past is conjured up in order to affect the political present.

Like the other prestige TV programs I have examined, *Game of Thrones* presents a reactionary backlash ideology within the context of a centrist metafiction.[7] However, unlike the other shows that mostly use aesthetic devices like direct addresses to the audience or oblique camera angles, this program enlists our knowledge of the past to place present ideas in a contradictory context that itself becomes doubled.[8] After all, the series is not a straightforward depiction

DOI: 10.4324/9781003352600-7

of the historical past; rather, it reconstructs the past from the perspective of the present as it conforms to Freud's notion that we always understand traumatic events through a retroactive process.[9]

The fundamental traumas that the show has at its center are the fall of pre-modern patriarchy and the threat of climate change. Within this cultural fantasy space, the attacking women, led by Daenerys with her dragons, represent the fear of the maternal super-ego.[10] This attacking entity is both a symbol of the threat of female power to male dominance and the embodiment of parental demands without the shelter of the paternal ideal.[11] As a fantasized figure driven by a defensive backlash psychology and politics, the freer of slaves and other oppressed groups is presented as a deadly, castrating force.[12] However, this underlying fantasy structure is repressed by the writers and the directors through the use of indirect symbolism. Furthermore, the audience is constantly being internally divided by the combination of the present and the past on one level and truth and fiction on another level.

As divided subjects enjoying our guilty pleasure, we are both attracted to and repulsed by the series' excess.[13] While we might fantasize about engaging in such extreme acts of violence, sexuality, and profanity, we are also horrified by the lack of social and individual restraint.[14] Although we do know that people in power can act in ways that the people without power are punished and disciplined for, we also envy the freedom and enjoyment of the dominant group.[15] Yet, as Jean Baudrillard reminds us, this sense of freedom and liberation is only a simulation produced by the culture industry with no other guiding aim than to attract attention and make money.[16] The series, then, has to manipulate the audience not only to get them to desire to watch the show, but it also has to motivate people to keep watching in an immersive and addictive manner.[17]

Through the use of cliffhangers and political intrigue, the desire of the audience is heightened as their drive for pleasure is satiated through escapism. By placing our current political desires and anxieties within a fictional representation of the past, we are able to remove ourselves from reality as our unconscious fears and desires are activated.[18] Moreover, the series reveals how through the power of art, every reality can be reshaped, including our collective history and memory. Since what in part defines prestige TV is its gritty realism, what we like about the series is that it is able to make the past come alive by projecting the present back in time.[19] Moreover, this displacement of the present gender war is doubled by an allegorical reference to climate change through the threat that "winter is coming."[20]

Rape and Revenge

One can read much of the unfolding of the narrative as a rape and revenge plot.[21] Thus, during the first few seasons, women are constantly being shown as prostitutes and victims of sexual assault. While the show cashes in on undressing attractive females, it leaves most of the violence to the armored males.[22] However, by the last two seasons, several women seeking revenge gain power as they become transformed from sexual objects to action figures.[23] Not only do we have the "mother of dragons," but the Stark females (Arya, Sansa) become more powerful as the evil Cersei plots her way to the top. This group of avenging females is coupled with a group of emasculated men—the imp, the cripple, the eunuch, and the bastard.[24]

We can certainly see the post-modern return of the oppressed as representing a Leftist reversal of premodern conservative culture; however, the murder of the mother of dragons at the end points to the way this threatening female power has to be produced in a hyperbolic way so that she can be later destroyed.[25] As a reactionary male fantasy, the horrific menace of female power requires a concerted effort to eliminate this dangerous force.[26] However, we should not focus on only the end point of the narrative because it is the underlying fantasy that often sustains the audience's attention. In fact, the contradictory subjectivity of centrist narcissism is presented through the coupling of an explicit post-modern, Leftist gender revolution and the use of implicit traditional conservative gender stereotypes.[27]

Bran the Broken

At the same time that the show presents the rise and revenge of powerful female figures, it traces the narrative of the youngest Stark son, Bran.[28] In the first season, we watch as Bran becomes crippled after he is pushed off a building when viewing Cersei and Jamie Lannister having sex.[29] In this re-enactment of a primal scene, the boy becomes castrated because he has witnessed an act of royal incest.[30] However, his punishing disability gives him access to supranatural powers and the ability to see both the past and the future.[31] In this strange mystification of castration and disability, it is the embodiment of castration caused by viewing the primal scene that enables Bran to ultimately be named king. Perhaps he is chosen because he shows no desire for the position, but the underlying message appears to be that only a castrated male can be trusted with power.[32]

Brandon the Broken is, therefore, both a victim and product of the female revolution and the symbol of the punishment for the illicit viewing of sex.[33] Through the unconscious use of primary processes, the audience is itself identified with this figure who is caught watching a scene of sexual deviance.[34] Although it is Jamie and Cersei who are committing incest, the viewing boy is the one who is punished and then later rewarded.[35] From a Freudian perspective, we can argue that Bran is punished for his own incestuous desires that are projected onto others through the imagination of traumatic primal scene. However, this pre-oedipal fantasy must be understood through the lens of a reconstructed past.

The Fall of Patriarchy

The series, then, titillates its audience by showing scenes of unconstrained sex and violence, but this spectacle also calls for punishment and castration.[36] In other words, the series not only caters to our libertarian desire for total freedom

92 *Game of Thrones*

and enjoyment, but it also provides access to castration as we are punished for viewing the primal scene. This narrative logic can be understood through Lacan's theory that patriarchy and the conservative social order are based on replacing the desire of and for the mother with what he calls the name-of-the-father.[37] For the early Lacan, the imposition of the paternal metaphor has a pacifying effect because the conflict between parents and the child is resolved by the acceptance of a third mediating term.[38] The paternal metaphor then stops the flow of metonymic maternal desire as the child identifies with the punishing, castrating father who embodies the law and the symbolic social order.[39]

According to this conservative theory, when the father's law is resisted or rejected, the maternal desire is no longer contained as the child has no way of symbolizing the irrational demands of the mother or containing his or her own drives.[40] We can read this theory as reflecting changing family structures and the feminist revolt against premodern patriarchy. With the father losing his position as the all-powerful law-giver and family monarch, the mother is no longer constrained, and the child is no longer cut off from the satisfaction of his or her desires.[41] As a metaphor for the "permissive society," the loss of the castrating paternal order results in the anxiety of desire without limits.[42]

In his later work, Lacan will rebel against his own earlier theory by focusing on how we are driven to enjoy at all costs as we realize that the symbolic Other does not really exist since he is just a social construction.[43] Similar to Marx's notion that modern capitalism dissolves the premodern social hierarchy and value system, Lacan points to the ways that jouissance (orgasm, enjoyment, pleasure) is in opposition to symbolic castration and the paternal order.[44] Thus, in a culture catering to the enjoyment of the viewing audience, we encounter the dominance of drives over social order.[45]

Although the ending of the series may indicate that castration has to be accepted as the disabled male son becomes king, we have to remember that our visual pleasure was first stimulated by a sexist social hierarchy followed by its feminist reversal. As an ideological construction creating an imaginary reconciliation out of social contradictions, the centrist fantasy underlying this show brings together desire and punishment as the audience is positioned to identify both with the aggressor and the victim.[46]

The Centrist Contradiction

In political terms, the centrist compromise points to the contradictory endorsement of women's rights and the repressed desire to maintain masculine dominance.[47] For the obsessional narcissist, every conformity to a rule is coupled with an underlying desire to be an exception.[48] Since one can only access enjoyment on an illicit level, fantasy becomes the place to experience sexual and violent impulses.[49] However, these desires are always treated as a taboo because they are objects of both attraction and repulsion; prestige TV then delivers guilty pleasure to a divided and conflicted audience that fears what it desires and desires what it fears.[50] Of course, social stability relies on this internalization of the super-ego, which as Freud indicates gains its power from the id, even though the conscience seeks to punish and censor these drives.[51]

It is just simply impossible to understand popular culture and our political affiliations if we do not comprehend how the unconscious use of primary processes structures our social order and individual reactions to that order.[52] Since we view ourselves and the world around us primarily through the lens of fantasy, we need to become aware of how our repressed imagination perceives reality. Instead of relying on the mystical projections of the present onto the past, we have to learn how to separate fiction from the real. Moreover, by constantly telling us that "winter is coming," the series presents the threat of climate change on a mythical and displaced level.[53] Like so many other social issues reflected in this cultural fantasy, the placement of real problems in a fictional context coupled with magical beings serves the function of mystifying our own reality.

Game of Thrones, then, not only makes a fictional past appear real and present, but it makes our own present seem unreal and fictional. Since the centrist subject is driven to avoid all feelings of shame, guilt, and anxiety, this show is a perfect vehicle for presenting, displacing, and containing our anti-social impulses and fears concerning our future demise.[54] While the last season of the series does provide the hope that people will come together to fight against an existential threat to the human race, this final political fantasy still relies on magic and mysticism to reverse the threat of both the coming winter and the mother of dragons. In fact, the attempt to present a realistic representation of magical beings reveals the real, underlying impetus of the show as fantasy becomes alive through artistic expertise.[55]

Gentrifying TV

As Dan Hassler-Forest argues in his "*Game of Thrones*: Quality Television and the Cultural Logic of Gentrification," the marketing of this series as prestige TV represents a form of cultural gentrification: "this transformation of media value constitutes a politics of adaptation that revolves around appealing to a desirable global elite audience through elaborate processes of branding and gentrification" (162).[56] Just as certain urban neighborhoods are transformed by attracting upscale dwellers, we can think of the production and marketing of prestige TV as a way of converting older forms of mass media and culture into symbols of an elite class. In the case of *Game of Thrones*, the low-brow genre of young male fantasy fiction is appropriated and adapted as a form of high art.[57] Hassler-Forest connects this cultural gentrification to the need for cable channels to cater to a high-paying, upper-middle-class audience:

> As network audiences declined in the face of competition from the proliferation of cable and satellite channels in the 1980s, the networks became less concerned with attracting mass audiences and increasingly concerned with retaining the most valuable audiences: affluent viewers that advertisers

were prepared to pay the highest rates to address. In other words, the compulsiveness of 'must see' television is designed to appeal to affluent, highly educated consumers who value the literary qualities of these programs, and they are used by the networks to hook this valuable cohort of viewers into their schedules. (162)

The changing nature of the television economy then allowed for cable channels to cater to an upscale, niche audience willing to pay for quality entertainment, and just like how low-rent neighborhoods are transformed when wealthy people seek to live in a place that is artsy or edgy, prestige TV sought to gentrify the low-status world of network TV by turning low culture into high culture.[58]

In comparing the adaptation of fantasy fiction to urban gentrification, Hassler-Forest reveals the class bias central to these transformations:

> This concept of 'Quality TV' is constructed around the notion of appealing to a particular audience with abundant disposable income, and has traditionally been organized around hybrid texts that combined familiar television formats with themes and aesthetics drawn from more celebrated sources such as the Hollywood gangster film, romantic comedy, and European arthouse cinema. Following the basic format established in the early 1980s by production company MTM, HBO was the first cable TV company to foreground its programming's high art connections by emphasizing "character development, structural complexity, reflexivity, [and] aesthetic innovation." (163)

Quality TV is here another name for prestige TV as both labels indicate a distinction between normal, low-class entertainment and elite, high-class culture.[59] Not only did these shows have to utilize certain aesthetic features to qualify as high art, but they also had to promote and advertise their aesthetic value.[60] In the same way that selective universities advertise their exclusive value through expensive marketing campaigns, prestige TV relies on marketing itself to the top 9.9%.[61] As Bourdieu insists, this marketing of value is based on conceptions of class and is not a natural occurrence since it requires extensive education and culture.[62]

Of course, the production and conception of prestige TV rely on associating the devalued realm of network television to the valorized forms of cinema and literature:

> television's strategic incorporation of elements from other media occurred within a context in which all narrative media were fully engaged in a complex process of technological and cultural convergence. Jim Collins describes the resulting alignment between cinema and literature as a new kind of 'cine-literary culture,' allowing for 'an unprecedented interdependency of the publishing, film, and television industries, which can reach that "public at large" wherever it may be with ever greater proficiency'. The

flattening out of former cultural hierarchies therefore results in an environment in which changing social practices alongside the increasing conglomeration of media industries has made the consumption of 'quality TV' a cine-literary experience that creates new value for corporate producers like HBO. (163–164)

The economic imperative behind the marketing of shows like *Game of Thrones* is therefore based on a class-based understanding of art since the goal of these media corporations is to motivate an upscale audience to purchase their services:

> This appeal hinges on HBO's identity as a premium brand offering boutique programming, perpetually constructing for itself 'an air of selectivity, refinement, uniqueness, and privilege'. For HBO and other television producers in the post-network era, the careful development of this brand identity has relied on the way in which it 'offers consumers a place where it's okay to be transgressive with regard to mainstream television.' (164).

What is so interesting about this assessment of class-based prestige TV is the claim that elite audiences want refinement and transgression. Similar to the wealthy people who move into a neighborhood full of artists, gay people, and trendy stores and restaurants, the bourgeois bohemians, so dear to David Brooks, want to combine together high-class values and low-class excitement.[63] Of course, the result of this process is that the starving artists and alternative people who first made the neighborhood trendy and cool are forced out because they can no longer afford the rent in the place they made attractive to the upper-middle class.[64] As we learned from Stewart's *The 9.9%*, this economic cohort takes advantage of inequality by increasing their wealth through homeownership and access to exclusive social institutions.[65]

Hassler-Forest's central argument, then, is that *Game of Thrones* helps the elite class to recognize and consolidate its own status, and part of the cost of this process is a devaluation of everything and anything that does not belong to this elite social group: "Premium cable's drama series tend to offer this kind of televisual transgression by including depictions of nudity, sex, and violence, alongside generous profanity, thus differentiating itself from 'normal' network TV drama and its traditional policy of offering 'least objectionable programming (LOP)'" (164). Elite status is tied here to anti-social behavior. In other words, the affluent signal their prestige not only through exclusivity but also transgression.[66] It is as if they show their wealth by having the extra resources to waste on consuming tabooed experience.[67] Similar to the notion of "slumming," the idea here is that the repressed desire of the elite class can only be accessed by watching someone else perform anti-social transgressions.[68]

This attraction to gratuitous depictions of sex, violence, and profanity matches the fascination centrists have with Right-wing politicians like Donald Trump.[69] One reason, then, why he received so much free media attention during his 2016

96 *Game of Thrones*

campaign was that mainstream centrist audience could not keep their eyes off of him as they were attracted to what repulsed them.[70] In a similar manner, when the upscale audience watches *Game of Thrones*, it is driven by the same compulsion to enjoy what it has learned to detest. The great trick of this show and other prestige TV is to flatter its audience for their exclusive aesthetic taste as their base impulses are gratified.[71] Thus, even as this high culture debases the low culture of network television, what really drives its success is its catering to de-valorized impulses.

Hassler-Forest insists that this combination of high culture and low impulses mimics the way the discredited genre of young male fantasy literature becomes gentrified:

> the series' systematic incorporation of brutal violence and explicit sex scenes thus functions not only to 'liberate television fiction from the laws governing established creative practices and writing styles', as is by now customary for premium cable productions; it also adapts the fantasy genre in a way that makes it more attractive and accessible to a very particular and explicitly adult audience, thus dramatically increasing its commodity value. (165)

This effort to increase the prestige and commercial value of prestige TV productions is once again centered on the ideological process of bringing together the virtues of aesthetic taste and the gratification of repressed anti-social drives. As Freud argues in relation to the underlying dynamics of obsessive-compulsive psychopathology, illicit desires have to be covered by rituals of purification.[72] In the case of *Game of Thrones*, the centrist audiences can purify their debased desires by placing them within the socially valorized context of high art. Meanwhile in political terms, this points to the way Democrats focus on their own careers and the careers of their professional donors and supporters as they pretend to be concerned about the common good. Since the 9.9% wants to exploit an unequal system but not feel guilty for excluding others, it has to signal its virtue through its consumption habits.

This focus on class also has a gender component: "This makes it irrelevant whether the actual audience is predominantly male or female: either way, the *dispositif* that defines the viewer's relationship to the medium has been changed from 'passive,' 'feminine' spectatorship to that of an 'active,' and therefore 'masculine' connoisseur" (166). Both the underlying drives and the idealization of aesthetic distance are coded as masculine, which serves to further differentiate prestige TV from the devalued realm of feminized mass spectatorship.[73] Therefore, even if *Game of Thrones* does relate a narrative of growing female power, it produces prestige by catering to the ideology of masculinized culture.

This gender conflict is, in turn, associated with an implicit racial and ethnic component on a symbolic level:

> The way in which these maps organize the narrative's physical and conceptual space into a basic binary distinction between the civilized world of Westeros and the more mystical, dangerous, and generally more primitive

areas to the east and south reflect a very specific tradition of the high fantasy genre that articulates a distinctly Eurocentric perspective. Visits to the foreign lands surrounding the central kingdoms of Westeros demonstrate the conventional forms of Orientalism, as both the non-Western geographies and their inhabitants are portrayed as mysterious, unchanging, backwards, and treacherous. Therefore, although *Game of Thrones* does not entirely duplicate Tolkien's more rampant xenophobia, the series' structural distinction between a Western 'us' and a mystical, foreign 'other' does clearly re-articulate the genre's traditional Eurocentric construction of global geopolitics. (168)

Although one can argue that the ultimate message of the show is that all people and cultures have to work together to fight climate change and save humanity, this global multi-cultural politics is coupled with the re-circulation of conservative and Right-wing prejudices and paranoia.[74] Once again, we witness here the doubled and contradictory nature of centrist psychopathology: opposite political positions are combined as progressive virtues serve to veil regressive investments.

Game of Thrones then relies on a set of classic premodern stereotypes and prejudices in order to build its fantasy-based allegory of our current political and social world:

> As Daenerys moves around the larger but far more thinly populated lands of Essos, she encounters several different cultures, many of which exist either as tribal hunter-gatherers (e.g. the Dothraki) or as vaguely Orientalist city-states (e.g. Qarth). What all the lands outside of Westeros have in common is that they are presented as more primitive and implicitly unchanging than the more advanced Seven Kingdoms. (169)

This opposition between the advanced, sophisticated West and the primitive, uncivilized East structure this fictional representation of the past through the lens of the present. Thus, even if the show eventually calls for all people to work together to fight the attack of the living dead, this message of global unity is framed by a racist and ethnocentric discourse.[75]

Due to its contradictory desire to be both progressive and conservative, the centrist middle ground ends up devaluing others as a false unity is proclaimed. In the case of *Game of Thrones*, the use of English as the universal language presents a form of global unity based on Western colonialization:

> The series' racial politics in relation to its spatial organization is even more pronounced in the television adaptation, where the 'Common Tongue' in Westeros is English while the inhabitants of Essos speak in made-up languages like 'High Vallyrian,' which are subtitled. The result is that the distinction between the 'normal' space of the kingdoms of Westeros, as a fantastical hybrid that fuses the British isles with continental Europe,

98 *Game of Thrones*

> systematically privileges the Eurocentric perspective over its available alternatives. While the series does go out of its way to cast its characters in such a way that none of these more 'primitive' lands can be directly related to a single real-world equivalent, the overall effect strongly reinforces the Orientalist conceit that projects a radical otherness onto the East. (169–170)

This presentation of English as the new universal language of the global elites can be related to how American media corporations are trying to become the common culture of the world's rich and educated classes.[76] Of course, the flip side of this universalization of the English language is the rendering of other cultures and people to a status of incomprehension. Premodern class, gender, and race hierarchies are here being circulated through a shared global media.

Following the old trope of liberal guilt and the white savior of primitive people, the show presents Daenerys as the only one who can free the slaves and save the devalued others: "The politics of this patronizing representation of non-Western spaces becomes most painfully obvious in the extended subplot of Daenerys's quest to liberate the slaves in several city-states in the southern region of Essos, located around Slaver's Bay. The motif of an enlightened 'white messiah' liberating non-Western cultures from their backward ways has a long history in Western literature and cinema" (170). At the heart of this white savior discourse, we find not only a devaluation of non-whites but also another way to repress guilt through virtue signaling.[77] In this contradictory fantasy, whites are not only shown to be the cause of oppression: They are also figured to be the solution.

As I have shown in my analysis of prestige TV, centrist politics, and the culture of narcissism, progressive narratives and values are often coupled with reactionary fantasies and investments: "In spite of *Game of Thrones'* aesthetic sophistication, narrative complexity, and adult sensibilities, the way it therefore maps out its world still tends to fall in line with a reactionary form of politics that privileges the Western perspective while applying generic but nevertheless egregious stereotypes to its imagined, non-Western 'other'" (170). This combination of sophistication and regressive stereotypes offers insight into the mindset of the 9.9%. As a subjectivity and class based on the narcissistic desire to hide illicit thoughts behind good intentions, the target audience requires a contradictory cultural experience.[78] For instance, *Game of Thrones* presents both regressive and progressive views of female characters:

> In its depiction of sex and (female) nudity, the series pays lip service to the books' cynical perspective on sex and the female body as a form of currency in its pseudo-medieval society. But more than this, several critics have pointed out that the show's constant flaunting of naked female bodies, quickly and astutely dubbed 'sexposition' by blogger and cultural critic Myles McNutt, has more to do with the kind of audience the series is addressing, and its obvious attempts to rid itself of those genre elements

that have limited high fantasy to a primarily fan-driven audience. Indeed, 'the show's softly lit and erotic staging of any scene involving a naked woman evokes Playboy of the 1960s and '70s more than it underscores sexual politics or a culture of violence'. At the same time, the series makes sure that it caters to progressive tastes and female viewers by including many women characters in non-traditional gender roles, including Brienne, Arya, and Daenerys. (171)

It is thus wrong to see the show as purely sexist or progressive because its main effect is to combine these opposite ideologies together in the form of a centrist compromise and neurotic symptom.[79] As Freud insisted, psychopathological symptoms are based on the contradictory combination of repression and fixation, and in the case of obsessive-compulsive neurosis, this bringing together of opposites is expressed through the object of desire, which is seen as repulsive, and the way that purification rituals try to shout down evil impulses.[80] Since obsessional narcissists want to see themselves as being good, they have to repress their anti-social desires, but since the repressed always returns, they often end up enjoying the guilt that is generated from their moral conscience on the level of imaginary fantasy.

In the next chapter, I will read *Succession* as a reversal of *Game of Thrones* because, in this later HBO series, it is not the magical past that comes alive, but the contemporary present is fictionalized. Once again, the question is what does the upper-middle-class audience get from these combinations of the past and the present and fiction and reality? Moreover, in the desire to name this mode of television prestigious, what do we learn about the role of class in determining aesthetic judgments?

Notes

1 Pavlac, Brian A., ed. *Game of Thrones versus history: written in blood*. John Wiley & Sons, 2017.
2 Clapton, William, and Laura J. Shepherd. "Lessons from Westeros: gender and power in Game of Thrones." *Politics* 37.1 (2017): 5–18.
3 Genz, Stéphanie. "'I'm not going to fight them, I'm going to fuck them': sexist liberalism and gender (A) politics in Game of Thrones." *Women of ice and fire: gender, Game of Thrones and multiple media engagements*. Bloomsbury, 2016: 243–66.
4 Digioia, Amanda. "The queen in the north: conceptualising international relations, popular culture, gender, and how feminine power won the Game of Thrones." *St Antony's International Review* 16.1 (2020): 116–146.
5 Harvey, Graham. *Animism: respecting the living world*. Columbia University Press, 2005.
6 Freud, Sigmund. *Totem and taboo*. Routledge, 2013.
7 Stankevičius, Armantas. *Elements of medieval history in non-historical fiction*. BS thesis. 2020.
8 Schwabe, Claudia. "The fairy tale and its uses in contemporary new media and popular culture introduction." *Humanities* 5.4 (2016): 81.
9 Bistoen, Gregory, Stijn Vanheule, and Stef Craps. "Nachträglichkeit: a Freudian perspective on delayed traumatic reactions." *Theory & Psychology* 24.5 (2014): 668–687.

10 Johnston, Adrian. "The vicious circle of the super-ego: the pathological trap of guilt and the beginning of ethics." *Psychoanalytic Studies* 3.3–4 (2001): 411–424.

11 Morris, Christopher D. "Reading the birds and The Birds." *Literature/Film Quarterly* 28.4 (2000): 250.

12 Samuels, Robert. "On the psychopathology of the new right: from Jurassic Park to the gendered culture wars." *New media, cultural studies, and critical theory after postmodernism.* Palgrave Macmillan, New York, 2009. 87–103.

13 Bergler, Edmund. "Three tributaries to the development of ambivalence." *The Psychoanalytic Quarterly* 17.2 (1948): 173–181.

14 Freud, Sigmund. *I. Creative writers and daydreaming.* Columbia University Press, 1983.

15 Costas, Jana, and Alireza Taheri. "'The return of the primal father' in postmodernity? A Lacanian analysis of authentic leadership." *Organization Studies* 33.9 (2012): 1195–1216.

16 Baudrillard, Jean. "Simulacra and simulations (1981)." *Crime and Media.* Routledge, 2019. 69–85.

17 Snyder, Rachael. "Binge on: the phenomenon of binge watching." Thesis (2016): https://digitalcommons.lasalle.edu/honors_projects/3

18 Biehl, Brigitte. "The 'Watching Dead'." *Organizational Aesthetics* 10.2 (2021): 8–11.

19 Carroll, Shiloh. *Medievalism in a Song of Ice and Fire and Game of Thrones.* Vol. 12. Boydell & Brewer, 2018.

20 Tarly, Samwell. "The climate of the world of Game of Thrones." *Philosophical Transactions of the Royal Society of King's Landing* 1.1 (2017): 1.

21 Elwood, Rachel L. "Frame of thrones: portrayals of rape in HBO's Game of Thrones." *Ohio St. LJ Furthermore* 79 (2018): 113.

22 Carroll, Shiloh. "Tone deaf?: Game of Thrones, showrunners and criticism." *HBO's Original Voices.* Routledge, 2018. 169–182.

23 Turner, Rachel. *The rhetoric of rape-revenge films: analyzing violent female portrayals in media from a narrative perspective of standpoint feminism.* Diss. 2018: https://hdl.handle.net/1805/17424

24 Johnston, Susan. "Abjection, masculinity, and sacrifice: the Reek of Death in Game of Thrones." *Men and Masculinities*(2021): 1097184X211044184.

25 Faludi, Susan. *Backlash: The undeclared war against American women.* Crown, 2009.

26 Hannell, Briony. "Controversy, sexual violence and the critical reception of Game of Thrones 'unbowed, unbent, unbroken'." Dissertation *University of East Anglia* (2016): 1–41.

27 Ucan, Aylin. *"Tears aren't a woman's only weapon, the best one's between your legs": postfeminist conceptions of gender and power in the American TV Series Game of Thrones.* Diss. Carl von Ossietzky Universität Oldenburg, 2017.

28 Ellis, Katie M. "Cripples, bastards and broken things: disability in Game of Thrones." *M/C Journal* 17.5 (2014) : 1.

29 Evans, Tania. "Cripples and bastards and broken things: masculinity, violence, and abjection in A Song of Ice and Fire and Game of Thrones." (2019): http://hdl.handle.net/1885/160822

30 Donnelly, Colleen Elaine. "Re-visioning negative archetypes of disability and deformity in fantasy: wicked, maleficent, and Game of Thrones." *Disability Studies Quarterly* 36.4 (2016).

31 Silverman, Eric J., and Robert Arp, eds. *The ultimate Game of Thrones and philosophy: you think or die.* Vol. 105. Open Court, 2016.

32 Sharland, S. "Bran the broken: classical precedents for the figure of bran stark in GRR Martin's A Song of Ice and Fire novels and in the game of thrones television series." *Akroterion* vol. 64 (2019): 145–167.

33 Haywood, Loraine. "Queen of the Ashes." *Woke Cinderella: Twenty-First-Century Adaptations.* Lexington, 2020. 97.

34 Blum, Harold P. "On the concept and consequences of the primal scene." *The Psychoanalytic Quarterly* 48.1 (1979): 27–47.

35 Keen, Helen. *The science of Game of Thrones: from the genetics of royal incest to the chemistry of death by molten gold-sifting fact from fantasy in the Seven Kingdoms.* Hachette UK, 2016.

36 Goldberg, Carl. "The shame of Hamlet and Oedipus." *Psychoanalytic Review* 76.4 (1989): 581–603.

37 Lacan, Jacques, Alan Sheridan, and Malcolm Bowie. *The agency of the letter in the unconscious or reason since Freud.* Routledge, 2020.

38 Forrester, John. "The Seminar of Jacques Lacan: in place of an introduction. Book II. The ego in Freud's Theory and in the Technique of Psychoanal." *Free Associations* 1.11 (1988): 86–107.

39 Fuchsman, Kenneth. "What does Freud mean by the Oedipus complex?." *Free Associations* 9.1 (2001): 82–118.

40 Ragland-Sullivan, Ellie. "The paternal metaphor: a Lacanian Theory of language." *Revue Internationale de Philosophie. Vol. 46:180* (1992): 49–92.

41 Thormann, Janet. "Lacan and the matter of origins." *Literature and Psychology* 47.1/2 (2001): 109.

42 Kilminster, Richard. "Narcissism or informalization? Christopher Lasch, Norbert Elias and social diagnosis." *Theory, Culture & Society* 25.3 (2008): 131–151.

43 Lacan, Jacques. *The seminar of Jacques Lacan: Book XX: Encore: 1972–1973.* Norton, 2011.

44 Voruz, Véronique, and Bogdan Wolf, eds. *The later Lacan: an introduction.* SUNY Press, 2012.

45 Samuels, Robert. "Catharsis: the politics of enjoyment." *Zizek and the rhetorical unconscious.* Palgrave Macmillan, Cham, 2020. 7–31.

46 Hirst, Paul Q. "Althusser and the theory of ideology." *Economy and Society* 5.4 (1976): 385–412.

47 Genz, Stéphanie. "Third way/ve: the politics of postfeminism." *Feminist Theory* 7.3 (2006): 333–353.

48 Freud, Anna. "Obsessional neurosis: a summary of psycho-analytic views as presented at the congress." *International Journal of Psycho-Analysis* 47 (1966): 116–122.

49 Poscheschnik, Gerald. "Game of Thrones—a psychoanalytic interpretation including some remarks on the psychosocial function of modern TV series." *The International Journal of Psychoanalysis* 99.4 (2018): 1004–1016.

50 Spanò, Carmen. "The attractions of 'Recoil' TV: the story-world of Game of Thrones." *The M in CITAMS@ 30.* Emerald Publishing Limited, 2018.

51 Freud, Sigmund. "The ego and the id (1923)." *TACD Journal* 17.1 (1989): 5–22.

52 Samuels, Robert. *The psychopathology of political ideologies.* Routledge, 2021.

53 DiPaolo, Marc. *Fire and snow: climate fiction from the Inklings to Game of Thrones.* Suny Press, 2018.

54 Samuels, Robert. "Transference and narcissism." *Freud for the twenty-first century.* Palgrave Pivot, Cham, 2019. 43–51.

55 Riggs, Don. "Continuity and transformation in the religions of Westeros and Western Europe." *Game of Thrones versus History: Written in Blood. Wiley,* 2017. 171–184.

56 Hassler-Forest, Dan. "Game of Thrones: Quality television and the cultural logic of gentrification." *TV/Series* 6 (2014: https://doi.org/10.4000/tvseries.323

57 Swirski, Peter, and Tero Eljas Vanhanen. "Introduction—browbeaten into pulp." *When highbrow meets lowbrow.* Palgrave Macmillan, New York, 2017. 1–9.

58 Zukin, Sharon. "Gentrification: culture and capital in the urban core." *Annual Review of Sociology* 13.1 (1987): 129–147.

59 McCabe, Janet, and Kim Akass. *Quality TV: contemporary American television and beyond.* Bloomsbury Publishing, 2007.

60 Bourdaa, Melanie. "This is not marketing. This is HBO: branding HBO with transmedia storytelling." *Networking Knowledge: Journal of the MeCCSA Postgraduate Network* 7.1 (2014).

61 McCabe, Janet, and Kim Akass. *It's not TV, it's HBO's original programming: producing quality TV.* Routledge, 2009.

62 Murdock, Graham. "Pierre Bourdieu, distinction: a social critique of the judgement of taste." *International Journal of Cultural Policy* 16.1 (2010): 63–65.

63 Brooks, David. *Bobos in paradise: the new upper class and how they got there.* Simon and Schuster, 2010.

64 Smith, Neil, and Peter Williams, eds. *Gentrification of the city.* Routledge, 2013.

65 Stewart, Matthew. "The 9.9 percent is the new American aristocracy." *The Atlantic* (2018).

66 Kakkar, Hemant, Niro Sivanathan, and Matthias S. Gobel. "Fall from grace: the role of dominance and prestige in the punishment of high-status actors." *Academy of Management Journal* 63.2 (2020): 530–553.

67 Harris, Marvin. "Potlatch." *Annual Edition: Anthropology* 91 (1990): 88–93.

68 Post, Jonathan Vos. "Towards enumeration of all possible economic systems." *Essays in Economic and Business History* 14 (1996): 441.

69 Fuchsman, Ken. "The presidential campaign that astounded the world: a psychohistory of Donald Trump and the 2016 American election." *The Journal of Psychohistory* 44.4 (2017): 292.

70 Lawrence, Regina G., and Amber E. Boydstun. "What we should really be asking about media attention to Trump." *Political Communication* 34.1 (2017): 150–153.

71 Stubbs, Andrew. "The Knick: a convergence between exploitation cinema, independent film, and Quality TV?." (2017).

72 Freud, Sigmund. "Notes upon a case of obsessional neurosis." *The Standard Edition of the complete psychological works of Sigmund Freud, Volume X (1909): two case histories ("Little Hans" and the "Rat Man").* Simon and Schuster, 1955. 151–318.

73 Trejo Morales, Cristina. "Non-conforming femininity in Game of Thrones: an analysis of Arya Stark and Brienne of Tarth." *Stacey Scriver and Carol Ballantine* 21 (2020): 7.

74 Wolfson, Todd. "The dark reality of fantasy: hegemonic oppression in 'Game Of Thrones' Daniel H. Corey Rutgers, The State University of New Jersey Media & Popular Culture." (2016): https://www.academia.edu/28036898/The_Dark_Reality_of_Fantasy_Hegemonic_Oppression_In_Game_Of_Thrones_

75 Downes, Stephanie, and Helen Young. "The maiden fair: nineteenth-century medievalist art and the gendered aesthetics of whiteness in HBO's Game of Thrones." *Postmedieval* 10.2 (2019): 219–235.

76 Rebane, Gala. "'There is no word for thank you in Dothraki': language ideologies in Game of Thrones." *Multilingualism in Film.* Peter Lang, 2019.

77 Schupbach, Jillian. "Dethroning the white savior: examining the characterization of Daenerys Targaryen in Game of Thrones from a postcolonial perspective." *Michigan Academician* 47.3 (2021): 105–115.

78 Samuels, Robert. "(Liberal) narcissism." *Routledge handbook of psychoanalytic political theory.* Routledge, 2019. 151–161.

79 Gjelsvik, Anne, and Rikke Schubart, eds. *Women of ice and fire: gender, Game of Thrones and multiple media engagements.* Bloomsbury Publishing USA, 2016.

80 Samuels, Robert. "Beyond Hillary Clinton: obsessional narcissism and the failure of the liberal class." *Psychoanalyzing the Left and Right after Donald Trump.* Palgrave Macmillan, Cham, 2016. 31–59.

8

CONCLUSION

Succession and the Metafictional Political Present

I conclude this analysis of the hidden politics and psychopathology of prestige TV by looking at HBO's *Succession*. What makes this series such a good candidate for summing up my arguments is that the show directly represents the relation between media and political ideology since it portrays a fictional depiction of the Right-wing news mogul Rupert Murdoch.[1] Framed as an updated version of *King Lear*, the fight over what sibling will take over this media empire represents another meta-fictional product from the "liberal" media.[2] In examining the centrist obsession with libertarian ideology, we see how Right-wing politicians like Donald Trump are often fortified by people who claim to detest every aspect of this political counter-revolution. In other words, I seek to argue that the Democrats have helped to create the contemporary Republican Party not only by ignoring the working class in favor of professional elites, but centrist media has fed the Right through the creation of cultural fantasies that both demonize and idealize anti-social libertarian ideology.[3]

It could appear to be absurd to seek to blame the sorry state of our politics on products of popular culture, but it should be clear that I am not pointing to an organized or even conscious conspiracy. Instead, by looking at the psychopathology of liberal centrists, I seek to expose how the circulation of unconscious cultural fantasies shape political realities.[4] The reason, then, why psychoanalysis is so essential to this project is that we have to account for a mode of communication that is indirect, unintentional, and unaware. Moreover, since fiction-based television series are supposed to show and not tell, there is a tendency to use the rhetorical devices of metaphor and association. Like a dream, everything that is represented can be read as representing something else.[5] Furthermore, due to the fact that logical relations cannot be expressed directly through images, the use of visual language requires a mode of interpretation that is aware of how to translate symbols into related meanings.

DOI: 10.4324/9781003352600-8

104 Conclusion

One of the great paradoxes of the shows that I have examined is that they combine gritty realism with ironic awareness. What is paradoxical about this form is that realism usually requires an immersive focus, while irony creates distance and a lack of immersion.[6] The trick then of these programs is that they have to appear believable, at the same time, they allow the audience to dissociate from what they are internalizing. Through a set of aesthetic signals, the audience is able to invest in anti-social actions and characters while still escaping any sense of guilt or shame. Thus, even when someone identifies with a character, they always know that what they are watching is not actually true and real. This creates a split form of subjectivity as one is both identifying and dis-identifying with the representations that combine fiction with reality.

The ultimate effect is to train people to divide their consciousness between social conformity and anti-social disinvestment. For instance, Freud found that obsessive-compulsive neurotics would perform private and public rituals of purification in order to cleanse themselves, literally or figuratively, of the shame and guilt caused by their anti-social desires.[7] However, the flip side of this shouting down of evil impulses was a tendency to fantasize about the very transgressions they were trying to repress. In a vicious circle, the more one gives up on one's desires, the more one feeds the super-ego, and thus the more one feels guilty and ashamed.[8] At the same time, the more rigid and demanding the super-ego becomes, the more one desires to transgress the internalized social law.[9]

It is this model of obsessive-compulsive neurosis that I am applying to the "liberal" audience of "liberal" media.[10] Moreover, the reason why I have to place liberal in quotation marks is that I do not think these contemporary liberals really represent the values and principles of modern liberal democracy. Instead of being invested in equality, truth, and impartiality, liberalism today is often defined by an obsessive-narcissistic desire to conform to the moralizing virtues of the Left while secretly desiring to transgress those super-ego demands. Thus, upper-middle-class centrists like to watch news shows that seek to promote political correctness and minority-based identity politics, and they also watch prestige TV fiction-based programs catering to the fantasy of total individual freedom and enjoyment.[11]

One of the major causes for the divided subjectivity and politics of centrists is that they seek to profit from inequality on a personal level as they bemoan it on a public level.[12] As the party of the professional elites, the underlying drive is a hyper-individualistic form of careerism, where all that really matters is to outcompete others in a system that is known to be corrupt and unequal.[13] Since they cannot imagine an alternative to the current capitalistic model, all they can do is conform from a position of ironic distance.[14] Furthermore, even though the Democrats have stopped providing effective policies to help most people of color, they still need to pretend they care about these people in order to gain their votes.[15] Luckily for the Democrats, the Republicans are so much worse for most minority groups that it does not matter how much the Democrats take these voters for granted. Likewise, while the Left does appear to care about the working class and minorities, their focus on race and gender has alienated many of the people they seek to help.[16] Instead of promoting the modern liberal democratic ideal of equality and impartiality, the Left has often taken on the position of the moral censor intent on shaming and canceling anyone who fails to speak and act in the right way.[17] Although we do need these Leftist social movements to make society more just and fair, the goal should be to expand who is covered by universal principles and not simply rejecting equality and impartiality under the banner of particular group identities.

The Politics of *Succession*

One of the interesting aspects of *Succession* is that the children represent these different, competing political ideologies. While the oldest son, Connor, mouths strongly libertarian ideas, his sister, Shiv, starts off working for a Left-of-center politician who seeks to take down the family's Right-wing media empire.[18] Meanwhile, Kendall, at times, appears to be very progressive, while at other times, he flirts with far-Right politics.[19] In contrast, the other son, Roman, tends to represent the ironic lens framing the show itself.[20] Through his constant joking and comic movements, Roman upsets the realism of the series as he caters to the split subjectivity of centrist Democrats.

In many ways, Logan Roy, the father and the owner of the corporation, presents the dying, old conservative order.[21] Like Lear, he needs to pick a successor, but Logan seems more interested in playing games with his children and forcing them to compete against each other for his recognition and love. Since he runs a family-owned business, he portrays mostly an older model of capitalism as his children seek to drag him into a new age of digital capital and shareholder finance.[22] At the same time, there is a haunting presence in the series, which is a group of criminal acts that have been covered up and risk being exposed. At the center of the scandal is sexual assault, and a relative, Lester, known as Moe, whose nickname we learn is short for molester. Similar to the sexual allegations brought against Rupert Murdoch's Fox News, the program relates masculine power to sexual wrong-doing.[23]

The Metafictional Present

A key aspect to this show is that it fictionalizes real people and events, which causes a metafictional doubling.[24] Not only is the series a representation of media reflecting on media, but the use of real politicians and journalists further blurs the line between fact and fiction. Like so many other prestige TV shows, the employment of self-reflexive metafiction allows the audience to take two opposed positions at the same time: on one level, the show is an accurate depiction of Fox News, and on another level, it can be read as a purely fictional representation with no direct connection to the real world.

In terms of politics, the use of metafictional techniques points to a divided subjectivity and a doubled, ironic discourse. Like the obsessional centrists who say one thing but act in another contradictory way, the series itself sends two opposing messages simultaneously. In fact, the use of humor in the show is often centered on

106 Conclusion

the way characters, like Tom, will say one thing and then immediately take it back and qualify it.[25] This self-negating discourse points to this character's compromised position and his need to both protect his own career and maintain the support of his wife, Shiv, who may or may not have his best interests at heart.

Another character who constantly contradicts himself in an open way is Roman, who is also trying to promote himself as he keeps performing acts of self-sabotage. In many ways, he is the family clown who cannot help putting his foot in his mouth and exposing his body in inappropriate ways.[26] Similar to so many of the other prestige TV shows, Roman's speech is full of profanity and transgressive allusions. In fact, his elaborate puns and references have the effect of bringing out the writing behind the speech since there is no way that someone could come up with such complicated wordplay in a spontaneous conversation.

In the mouths of these characters, simple phrases are subverted through hostile and sexual suggestions. As a symptomatic return of the repressed, whatever these characters are hiding from themselves and each other returns in a verbally disguised way. Following Freud's theory of aggressive humor, we see how the obsessional desire to hide hostile and sexual impulses results in a displaced mode of unconscious communication.[27] We can relate this indirect symbolic violence to the way politicians use coded language to express unacceptable ideas.[28]

The Primal Father

The figure who expresses his hostility in the most open way is Logan, who comes off of a Trump-like character prone to impulsive acts and extreme shifts between idealization and debasement.[29] From a psychoanalytic perspective, Logan represents the primal father who has direct access to sex and violence without social restraint.[30] Since Logan can always buy his way out of any problem, he does not have to control his drives, and so he remains relatively uncastrated. It is this image of the all-powerful male that often underlies libertarian politics.[31] In the quest for total freedom and enjoyment, any social restriction is seen as a threat of castration.[32] Thus, the desire to not pay taxes or have their businesses regulated pushes the Right to demonize government and debase progressive social movements. However, this contemporary tax revolt is often hidden by pandering to religious conservatives and the white working class.[33] Trading on a shared hatred of the Left and a reaction to a changing society where white Christian males no longer dominate as much, the Republican coalition is founded on a rhetorical misdirection.[34] To prevent supporters from focusing on class, cultural differences are highlighted in the form of a polarized culture war, which the "liberal" media then amplifies.[35]

As the owner of a Right-wing propaganda machine, Logan Roy often voices that he controls the president, and it is up to him to pick the new leader.[36] Logan's power, then, does not come primarily from his money but from his media influence. Since the media is positioned here to be the most powerful political entity, we have to ask what the show is saying about its own status as a media product. Is the series claiming that it has immense social power, or does it use humor and metafiction to free itself from any responsibility? The answer to these questions has to be both yes and no: The series reflects our political reality, but it also feeds the underlying fantasies that shape our ideological commitments.

Just as the obsessional Rat Man in Freud's case was fascinated by the story of a cruel captain who forced rats into people's rectums, the centrist audience has an extreme enjoyment watching powerful figures like Trump and Logan.[37] Moreover, Freud highlights that when the Rat Man recounts this story of a strange punishment, he shows an enjoyment that he was not aware of himself. This unconscious pleasure relates to our guilty pleasures and transgressive desires that are satisfied by cultural fantasies, which in turn normalize and empower sociopathic leaders.

It is important to highlight how unlike the other shows I have examined, with *Succession*, criminality is part of the corporate business world. There is thus no clear line between what is legal and what is illegal as modern capitalism is depicted as relying on hidden transgressive secrets. In this distrust of our economic system, the culture industry is able to position itself as both inside and outside of the capitalist world it critiques. Like the narcissistic centrists I have been examining, the series wants to make money as it decries the corrupting influence of compulsive capitalism. Since the goal of the obsessive-narcissistic centrist is to be seen as a good person with good intentions, any complicity with the system has to be repressed and displaced onto cultural fantasies.

Audience of One

As we have seen throughout this book, much of elite TV is shaped by an ironic take on cynical, anti-social libertarian anti-heroes. Not only do the shows themselves display this centrist approach to their subject matter, but most of the critics of these programs also present a doubled, contradictory response. For instance, in his *Audience of One*, James Poniewozik seeks to equate Trump's rise to power with the forms and sensibility of television itself:[38]

> It tells two parallel stories. One is about television: how TV culture changed from the era of midcentury media monoliths to the age of media bubbles, how it reflected and affected our relationships with society, with politics, with one another. The other is about Donald Trump: a man who, through a four-decades-long TV performance, achieved symbiosis with the medium. Its impulses were his impulses; its appetites were his appetites; its mentality was his mentality. (xvi)

This analysis of television and Trump tends to replicate the centrist debasement of television and the Right as it centers on the audience's fascination with dark, cynical anti-heroes:

> It's about how pop culture got louder and more abrasive, more comfortable with cheering for the antihero. It's about how the techniques of reality

108 Conclusion

> TV—conflict, stereotype, the fuzzy boundary between truth and fiction—
> became tools of politics. It's about how public fights were carried out through
> the pro-wrestling histrionics of cable news. It's about how the culture war
> originated as a proxy for politics and increasingly became politics itself.
> Through all of those changes, Donald Trump used the dominant media of
> the day—tabloids, talk shows, reality TV, cable news, Twitter—to enlarge
> himself, to become a brand, a star, a demagogue, and a president. (xvi–xvii)

The main problem I see with this analysis is that it does not distinguish between
the immersive techniques of news shows, reality TV, and wrestling on the one
hand and the use of aesthetic distance with prestige TV shows on the other hand.
In other words, it lumps together two different ideologies as it fails to take into
account the frame of its own perspective.

Centrists may love to criticize Trump and other Right-wingers, but they
also love to watch people who refuse to be censored or controlled by social
norms. Moreover, as I have been arguing, the critique of the Right by centrists
serves as a mode of purification as they signal their virtue by condemning
someone else's moral and ethical lapses. One effect of this structure is that the
upper-middle class does not have to admit their own role in destroying modern liberal democratic institutions because all of the blame is placed on the
destructive Right.

My goal here is not to absolve Republicans or to deny their destructive effects
on our society and politics; rather, I want to highlight another part of the story
that is often ignored or repressed. Since the world of critics and academic writers
is often shaped by the values of the centrist 9.9%, there is a tendency to focus
all criticism on conservatives, the Left, and the Right.[39] We also find a snobby
mocking of mass culture and the people who consume this debased product. In
fact, while the Right tends to see centrist as being fake and hypocritical, centrists usually present the Right as not really believing in what they are saying
and doing: "Like any other long-running public performance, the Trump character evolved—became more stylized, exaggerated, sharp-edged—but its constant was its understanding of the instinctual appetites and fears of its audience"
(xxiii). Poniewozik posits here that Trump, and the television shows viewed by
his supporters, are both a fake performance and an appeal to real, basic impulses.
Although this assessment may be mainly correct, it does not account for the fact
that prestige TV shows catering to centrist Democrats are also fictional representations dedicated to gratifying the anti-social impulses of the audience.
What this centrist critique leaves out is that what really differentiates these two
approaches is the elitist use of aesthetic distance.

The ironic signaling of distance in prestige TV has been shown to be an indi-
cation of class as the top 9.9% seek to reveal their ability to consume a product
that serves no necessary function.[40] Since these narcissists want to show off their
value by not being tied down to the necessities of life and economic survival,
they need to get others to recognize their gratuitous indulgences. As Bourdieu

insists, high art serves as a way of both reflecting and internalizing exclusivity and prestige. Of course, this selectivity, like an elite college, needs to produce its value by being scarce and by devaluing the competition.[41] Poniewozik's blindness to the role of scarcity in creating prestige is reflected in the following statement: "Television is as much the opposite of that business as can be. Real estate is the business of scarcity. Television is the business of ubiquity" (5). It would be more correct to say that certain forms of television function like real estate because their values are in part based on their scarcity. Since cable channels had to convince upscale people to buy their expensive subscriptions when they could get regular television for free, they needed to idealize their own productions as they cashed in on their exclusivity.[42]

This purchasing of exclusive experiences is very similar to the way the 9.9% parents invest in selective activities to get their children into elite universities. In fact, the same logic applies to wealthy neighborhoods, which are often associated with "good schools."[43] To help their children succeed, the educated elite build the resumes of these young people by having them engage in elite activities often related to exclusive sports (crew, lacrosse) and the high arts (violins, not drums).[44] Prestige then does not just grow on trees: It has to be purchased for a high cost. As Mathew Stewart insists, this use of resources to take advantage of a highly unequal society fuels the hypocrisy of the meritocracy: A system that is claimed to be fair and just has been rigged by the power of money to exploit comparative advantages. Meanwhile, this anti-social competition for elite status can be hidden by the centrist 9.9% by focusing all of the blame on the anti-social capitalists and libertarian Neoliberals.

I am arguing that it is not wrong to critique the selfish and destructive aspects of the Right, but what is counter-productive is to use the criticisms of Republicans in order to justify and rationalize the privilege and power of the centrist 9.9%, especially when that power relies on exploiting others and avoiding responsibility. By externalizing bad behavior so that it is only the other who is seen as acting anti-social or selfish, prestige TV and its critics end up repressing their own role in the destruction of the liberal democratic social contract. We see this problem in Poniewozik's comparison of the old show *Profit* and the new elite cable programs:

> Within a decade, the approach that made Profit a failure in 1996—what broadly speaking we call "antihero drama"—would become the default mode of some of television's best and most popular shows. The exploits of ruthless, charismatic men (with a few exceptions, it was largely men) occupied The Sopranos, Deadwood, and Breaking Bad. Mad Men's advertising executive Don Draper, like Jim Profit, was a troubled country boy who stole a man's identity; in business, his clinical amorality allowed him to understand his market on a primal level. Had the medium changed, or had the audience? As is often the case, each changed the other. (88)

110 Conclusion

I would not disagree that television shapes the audience and the audience shapes television, but it is essential to examine how the role of anti-heroes in prestige TV relies on a doubled, ironic centrist discourse.[45]

In discussing Tony Soprano, Poniewozik does indeed highlight how this complex anti-hero may not only represent someone like Donald Trump but also the television executives who help to promote and support the representation of this type of personality:

> There was a push-pull to him, as there was with many antiheroes. He was an indictment of male aggression and entitlement. But he was also a fantasy of it. As Brett Martin notes in his study of antihero drama, *Difficult Men*, Tony and the characters who came after him tended to be middle-aged white men with power and angst—very much like the TV executives who put these shows on the air. (94)

In pointing to the combination of power and angst in prestige TV anti-heroes, we get to see how the upper-middle class suffers from never having enough money or status.[46]

From Logan Roy to Donald Trump

While Poniewozik does not focus directly on Logan Roy, his analysis of Trump's reality TV show, *The Apprentice,* sounds like a description of how Trump ran his White House and how Logan Roy runs his company and family:

> AND WHAT IS THE GAME? Ostensibly, it's about business. But as the season goes on, boardroom after boardroom, it becomes clear that it is mostly about the ability to sell one's self. The challenges, which take up most of the episode, determine which team goes into the boardroom. But once the doors shut, it's often as if the challenge never happened. The boardroom becomes a pressure-cooker game in itself, where the object is to please the boss, undermine your colleagues, and find a more vulnerable teammate to sacrifice. (132–133)

In the case of *Succession*, each family member is trying to please their father, who is also the boss; however, Logan remains unpredictable and volatile. Like the 9.9% catering to the 0.1% masters of finance and business, the primal father can be irrational and inconsistent because everyone has to cater to him.

Poniewozik's apt description of Trump's behavior on his reality show provides insight into the depiction of Logan Roy:

> Facing Trump in the boardroom is like being trapped in a cage with a capricious monster. You don't know what he wants, what will anger him, or why, but it's your job to make sure he eats your adversary instead of

Conclusion **111**

you. The boardroom is like a platonic visualization of Trump's mindset. There is the idea, which he practiced in business and politics, that conflict, especially among teammates, is the most productive state of humanity. He loves to put contestants in prisoner's-dilemma situations, asking them in turn, "Who should go?" You could get in trouble for naming your opponent simply because they named you. You could get in trouble for not doing it. (133)

This pitting of individuals against each other reflects the way Logan Roy treats his family members and employees: He desires to see each person vie for his support by sacrificing everyone else. However, this description is not about Logan, it is about Trump, and so we must ask what does our understanding of Trump tell us about *Succession*, and what does *Succession* tell us about Trump?

While authoritarian leaders like Trump may act erratic and unpredictable, they are able to do so because of their power and the irrational devotion of their supporters.[47] When the only game in town is run by a mad king, you have to play the game as best as you can.[48] In fact, we can think of contemporary financial capitalism and media culture as both inherently crazy since they rely on volatility and viral feedback loops.[49] Since we never know if someone like Logan Roy is insane or just impulsive, we have to accept that the most powerful people do not have to be rational or consistent. As Trump said, he could shoot someone in the middle of Fifth Avenue, and he would not lose his supporters.[50] This level of irrational support relates to the way media outlets, like *Fox News*, have trained their audience to internalize any representation—no matter how irrational it might be.[51]

It is interesting that, like Trump, Logan Roy appears to have no real values or tastes. He may control a media company, but he himself acts as the pure master unconcerned with what others think, and it is in part this lack of values or concern that drives his children and employees mad.[52] For instance, when his children ask him if they did the right thing, he usually just shrugs or ends the conversation. For Poniewozik, this type of behavior can be seen as a way of keeping subordinates on their toes as they try to outcompete each other:

What seemed like bedlam from the outside—because it was—invigorated Trump, who believed, like a born reality-TV producer, that warfare and distrust were the most productive and entertaining modes of existence. If his team of suck-ups, throat-cutters, and toadies were constantly fighting among themselves, it meant that they were fighting for his favor—and that meant that he was the one who mattered, he was the sun who gave every flower life, and every day would be the Who Loves Father Best contest that he craved. (134–135)

Although Poniewozik is trying to understand Trump's behavior in politics and on his television show, his descriptions can be applied to Logan Roy if we remove the irony and humor, but it is the ironic frame that defines the show and its audience.[53]

112 Conclusion

As I have argued throughout this book, the centrist fascination with Trump and other anti-social personalities has to be understood through the narcissistic subjectivity of self-division.[54] While there is an unconscious identification with sociopathic behavior, this repressed fantasy is countered by aesthetic distance. In contrast to this internal division, the libertarian Right values the authenticity of the uncensored subject—even if what is said is untrue: "To be real is to be willing to offend, to tell someone off to their face, to 'say what's on your mind,' even if what's on your mind happens to be a lie" (135). This emphasis on keeping it real is something that the centrist critics and politicians tend to get wrong about Trump and other libertarian politicians: What their supporters admire is realness and not necessarily the truth.[55]

This desire for leaders to stay unscripted and authentic also relates to the acceptance of a lack of empathy and understanding.[56] In relation to The *Apprentice,* Poniewozik, points out that Trump's catchphrase revealed his essential meanness and disregard for others: "The show's fans especially loved his catchphrase, 'You're fired.' Which is to say, they loved the antihero who embodied the dream of living like a king and telling people that they sucked without worrying about hurt feelings or repercussions. This was always a key part of the Donald Trump character. Now it defined him" (136). People on the Right are then attracted to politicians and businessmen who directly express their power without regard for how they are affecting others. This celebration of the uncensored leader matches the desire for uncensored free speech and the opposition to political correctness.[57]

While centrists might like the gratuitous depiction of violence and sex because it feeds an unconscious identification with repressed impulses, the Right experiences expressions of anti-social behavior as a freedom from social control.[58] The Right then might experience Logan Roy telling someone to "Fuck Off" as an expression of free speech, while centrists laugh nervously at its unleashed aggression. As an extreme representation of an extreme character, Logan embodies the fundamental libertarian fantasy of total freedom and enjoyment.[59] He is the primal father and the mad king all rolled into one as his power and money free him from social niceties.

While *Succession* may be using Logan to mock Trump, its use of satire makes it unclear what we are supposed to take away from its depiction of Right-wing politics. Other than revealing the madness caused by extreme power and wealth, it is unclear what the audience should think. Interestingly, for Poniewozik, the main effect of understanding how Right-wing media and power function is to allow the centrist audience the ability to congratulate themselves for not being such easy dupes of television propaganda. In referring to Rodger Ailes and the creation of Fox News, he reiterates the stereotypical condemnation of the Right-wing media audience:

> Among the team Ailes assembled was Chet Collier, his old boss from *The Mike Douglas Show*, whom Ailes's biographer Gabriel Sherman quoted as telling producers: "Viewers don't want to be informed; they want to feel informed." Collier's aphorism was one word too long. Viewers wanted to feel, period. Feel angry. Feel scared. Feel gleeful. This was what Fox delivered. (152)

In a reversal of the usual cultural hierarchy valorizing masculine reason over feminine emotion, this centrist critique equates the mostly masculine *Fox News* audience with feelings in contrast to the informed, thinking viewers. This analysis does little to further understand why so many people buy into the lies circulated on Right-wing media. It is simply too reductionist and elitist to see these viewers as merely dupes controlled by their emotions alone.

My point is not to reject the need to criticize Right-wing leaders, media, and voters; instead, we have to try to comprehend the psychopathology behind this ideology without using our criticism to make us feel good about our moral superiority. In fact, Poniewozik's attempt to provide a deeper psychological explanation for Right-wing media and politics follows Hofstadter's old focus on paranoia and conspiracy thinking:

> "The modern right wing," Hofstadter wrote, "feels dispossessed: America has been largely taken away from them and their kind, though they are determined to try to repossess it and to prevent the final destructive act of subversion." Hofstadter argued that the right was more susceptible to this ideation because of its continual sense that the country was moving away from it. But he was not describing an ideology so much as a leitmotif. America was always inches away from the apocalypse in this recurring tune, whose notes were "heated exaggeration, suspiciousness, and conspiratorial fantasy." (146–147)

This focus on a sense of lost identity in a changing society is evident in Trump's call to Make America Great Again, and it also helps to explain aspects of the angry white male anti-heroes so common in prestige TV shows, but what is missed in this analysis is the way the super-wealthy have been able to increase their wealth by getting the white working class to support politicians bent on reducing taxes and the very government programs on which many of these voters rely.[60] Part of this process is clearly based on the ability to make Republicans hate Democrats, and some of the support comes from implicit, and at times explicit races, sexism, and homophobia, but little of this magic trick would work if the Right actually had a consistent and logical set of policies. Since Trump was an amoral opportunist, like Logan Roy, he could bring together Christian fundamentalists, libertarian free traders, military nationalists, and angry white men, and it did not matter if these different groups were really at odds with each other because what they really wanted was power.

Saving Democracy?

As we have seen in the analysis of prestige TV anti-heroes, the centrist response to anti-social personalities is to condemn them on a conscious level and identify with them on an unconscious level. Since obsessional narcissists are attracted to what repulses them and repulsed by what attracts them, their fantasies are contradictory and divided. In the case of *Succession*, all of the children are repulsed

114 Conclusion

by their father's behavior, but they also identify with him and want to take his place. This family of social climbers can be compared to the 9.9% who have undermined liberal institutions from the inside through their selfish careerism. However, the underlying capitalistic drive of these individuals is in part hidden in the series by the use of humor, irony, and metafiction.

To really comprehend how the upper-middle class is able to take advantage of a highly unequal society and still retain a self-image of being good and pure, it is necessary to understand the ways repression and narcissism function.[61] Not only do these elites lie to others about their true intentions, but they also lie to themselves. In order to escape feelings of guilt and shame, they need to cover their selfish acts and impulses with virtue signaling as a form of ritualistic moral purification. This gives these mostly Democrats the air of being hypocritical because they do not really believe in what they profess. Although one can argue that conservatives and Right-wingers pose the greatest threat to liberal democracy, what is often neglected is the way centrist liberals have undermined democracy from within.

It is my hope that liberal democracy can be saved by, in part, understanding the underlying fantasies supporting political ideologies. This process requires applying psychoanalytic concepts and methods to the analysis of popular culture and other products of the culture industry. Moreover, if we want to restore faith in our liberal institutions, we have to gain a better understanding of the values and principles supporting this modern social order. This process entails distinguishing between narcissistic centrists and liberal democracy since the myth of the "liberal" media distorts our view of both culture and politics.

Notes

1 Wald, Christina. "King Lear and Succession: returns of the predecessor." *Shakespeare's serial returns in Complex TV*. Palgrave Macmillan, Cham, 2020. 83–136.
2 Charpentier, Anton. *Neoliberalism in Prestige Television: a story of masculinity, gender, and finance*. Diss. University of Calgary, 2021.
3 Frank, Thomas. *Listen, liberal: or, what ever happened to the party of the people?*. Macmillan, 2016.
4 Samuels, Robert. *The psychopathology of political ideologies*. Routledge, 2021.
5 Freud, Sigmund. *The interpretation of dreams: the complete and definitive text*. Basic Books, 2010.
6 Hoel, Erik P. "Fiction in the age of screens." *The New Atlantis* (2016): 93–109.
7 Carr, Anthony T. "Compulsive neurosis: a review of the literature." *Psychological Bulletin* 81.5 (1974): 311.
8 Johnston, Adrian. "The vicious circle of the super-ego: the pathological trap of guilt and the beginning of ethics." *Psychoanalytic Studies* 3.3–4 (2001): 411–424.
9 Freud, Sigmund. *Civilization and its discontents*. Broadview Press, 2015.
10 Samuels, Robert. "Beyond Hillary Clinton: obsessional narcissism and the failure of the liberal class." *Psychoanalyzing the Left and Right after Donald Trump*. Palgrave Macmillan, Cham, 2016. 31–59.
11 Gómez-Peña, Guillermo. "Performing against the cultural backdrop of the mainstream bizarre." *The version of the essay published on La Pocha Nostra website*: http://www. pochanostra. com/antes/jazz_pocha2/mainpages/bizarre. htm.
12 Huntington, Samuel P. "American ideals versus American institutions." *Political Science Quarterly* 97.1 (1982): 1–37.

13 Constantino, Paul R., et al. "The birth of a New American Aristocracy: In June, Matthew Stewart wrote about the gilded future of the top 10 percent–and the end of opportunity for everyone else." *The Atlantic* 322.2 (2018): 8–10.

14 Fisher, Mark. *Capitalist realism: is there no alternative?*. John Hunt Publishing, 2009.

15 Frank, Thomas. *Listen, liberal: or, what ever happened to the party of the people?*. Macmillan, 2016.

16 Fraser, Steve. "It's time to take woke capital seriously." *Dissent* 69.1 (2022): 107–114.

17 Samuels, Robert. "Pathos, hysteria, and the left." *Zizek and the rhetorical unconscious.* Palgrave Macmillan, Cham, 2020. 33–47.

18 Murphy, Jack. "Succession." *Philosophy Now* 140 (2020): 46–47.

19 Frumkin, R.A. "Hearing is believing." *Resonance: The Journal of Sound and Culture* 2.1 (2021): 19–26.

20 Charpentier, Anton. *Neoliberalism in Prestige Television: a story of masculinity, gender, and finance.* Diss. University of Calgary, 2021.

21 Wald, Christina. "King Lear and Succession: returns of the predecessor." *Shakespeare's serial returns in Complex TV.* Palgrave Macmillan, Cham, 2020. 83–136.

22 Cox, Damian, and Michael P. Levine. "Good hate." *The Moral Psychology of Hate.* Rowman and Littlefield, 2021. 165.

23 Zinsmeister, Karl. "Rupert Murdoch." *The American Enterprise* 8.5 (1997): 20–25.

24 Brady-Brown, Annabel. "Greed is good." *Big Issue Australia* 616 (2020): 28–29.

25 Hirsch, Kasper. "A study on power relations in Succession: a conversation analysis approach to the study of power." (2020).

26 Brehas, Ivana. "The queer art of sitting." *Kill Your Darlings* (Jul–Dec 2020): 220–226: https://www.killyourdarlings.com.au/article/the-queer-art-of-sitting/

27 Freud, Sigmund. *Jokes and their relation to the unconscious.* W. W. Norton & Company, 1960.

28 Haney-López, Ian. *Dog whistle politics: how coded racial appeals have reinvented racism and wrecked the middle class.* Oxford University Press, 2015.

29 Foster, Hal. "Père Trump." *October* 159 (2017): 3–6.

30 McAdams, Dan P. "The appeal of the primal leader: human evolution and Donald J. Trump." *Evolutionary Studies in Imaginative Culture* 1.2 (2017): 1-13.

31 Brock, Maria. "The hyperrealities of Putin and Trump: why it is worth paying attention to the public personas of political leaders." *Baltic Worlds* 9.4 (2016): 83–87.

32 Samuels, Robert. "Trump and Sanders on the couch: neoliberal populism on the Left and the Right." *Psychoanalyzing the Left and Right after Donald Trump.* Palgrave Macmillan, Cham, 2016. 61–76.

33 Frank, Thomas. *Pity the billionaire: the hard-times swindle and the unlikely comeback of the right.* Macmillan, 2012.

34 Samuels, Robert. "Victim politics: psychoanalyzing the neoliberal conservative counter-revolution." *Psychoanalyzing the Left and Right after Donald Trump.* Palgrave Macmillan, Cham, 2016. 7–29.

35 Klein, Ezra. *Why we're polarized.* Simon and Schuster, 2020.

36 Tally, Margaret. *The limits of #MeToo in Hollywood: gender and power in the entertainment industry.* McFarland, 2021.

37 Freud, Sigmund. "Notes upon a case of obsessional neurosis." *The Standard Edition of the complete psychological works of Sigmund Freud, Volume X (1909): two case histories ("Little Hans" and the "Rat Man").* 1955. 151–318.

38 Poniewozik, James. *Audience of one: Donald Trump, television, and the fracturing of America.* Liveright Publishing, 2019.

39 Frank, Thomas. *Listen, Liberal: Or, what ever happened to the party of the people?.* Macmillan, 2016.

40 Alba, Richard, and Philip Kasinitz. "Sophisticated television, sophisticated stereotypes: The Sopranos (HBO), created by David Chase." *Contexts* 5.4 (2006): 74–77.

41 Samuels, Robert. *Educating inequality: beyond the political myths of higher education and the job market.* Routledge, 2017.

116 Conclusion

42 Newman, Michael Z., and Elana Levine. *Legitimating television: media convergence and cultural status*. Routledge, 2012.

43 Posey-Maddox, Linn, Shelley McDonough Kimelberg, and Maia Cucchiara. "Middle-class parents and urban public schools: current research and future directions." *Sociology Compass* 8.4 (2014): 446–456.

44 Rivera, Lauren A. *Pedigree*. Princeton University Press, 2016.

45 Lyons, Siobhan. "The (anti-) hero with a thousand faces: reconstructing villainy in The Sopranos, Breaking Bad, and Better Call Saul." *Canadian Review of American Studies* 51.3 (2021): 225–246.

46 Felski, Rita. "Nothing to declare: identity, shame, and the lower middle class." *PMLA* 115.1 (2000): 33–45.

47 Hibbing, John R. *The securitarian personality: what really motivates Trump's base and why it matters for the post-trump era*. Oxford University Press, 2020.

48 Parmar, Inderjeet. "Trump may seem crazy, but he is not (always) mad." *USApp-American Politics and Policy Blog* (2020).

49 Shiller, Robert J. *Irrational exuberance*. Princeton university press, 2015.

50 Locke, Jill. "Donald Trump is not a shameless toddler: the problems with psychological analyses of the 45th US President." *Krisis* 39.1 (2019): 37-45.

51 Jamieson, Kathleen Hall, and Joseph N. Cappella. *Echo chamber: Rush Limbaugh and the conservative media establishment*. Oxford University Press, 2008.

52 Faktorovich, Anna. "Theoretical film studies: comic and tragic television series." *Cinematic Codes Review* 5.1 (2020): 5–58.

53 Irwin, Andrew. "Too much pills and liquor: a monthly round-up of listening and watching." *TLS. Times Literary Supplement* 6073–6074 (2019): 27–28.

54 Johnson, Edward A., Norah Vincent, and Leah Ross. "Self-deception versus self-esteem in buffering the negative effects of failure." *Journal of Research in Personality* 31.3 (1997): 385–405.

55 Theye, Kirsten, and Steven Melling. "Total losers and bad hombres: the political incorrectness and perceived authenticity of Donald J. Trump." *Southern Communication Journal* 83.5 (2018): 322–337.

56 Schrock, Douglas, et al. "Signifying aggrieved white selves: Trump supporters' racial identity work." *Sociology of Race and Ethnicity* (2021): 23326492211020780.

57 Montgomery, Martin. "Post-truth politics?: authenticity, populism and the electoral discourses of Donald Trump." *Journal of Language and Politics* 16.4 (2017): 619–639.

58 Samuels, Robert. "Catharsis: the politics of enjoyment." *Zizek and the rhetorical unconscious*. Palgrave Macmillan, Cham, 2020. 7–31.

59 Samuels, Robert. "Victim politics: psychoanalyzing the neoliberal conservative counter-revolution." *Psychoanalyzing the Left and Right after Donald Trump*. Palgrave Macmillan, Cham, 2016. 7–29.

60 Frank, Thomas. *Pity the billionaire: the hard-times swindle and the unlikely comeback of the right*. Macmillan, 2012.

61 Samuels, Robert. "Transference and narcissism." *Freud for the twenty-first century*. Palgrave Pivot, Cham, 2019. 43–51.

INDEX

9.9%, The 1, 3, 10, 22–24, 28, 31, 56, 61, 63, 67–68, 70, 80, 94, 95, 96, 98, 102, 108–109, 110, 114

Aarons, Leslie A. 40
Abramowitz, Alan, and Ruy Teixeira 54
addiction 15, 18, 38, 47, 53, 58, 68, 90
Adorno, Theodor W., and Max Horkheimer 52
aesthetic distance 2, 5, 8, 9, 23, 32, 34, 45, 55–56, 69, 80, 83, 85, 96, 104, 108, 112
Aistrup, Joseph A. 53
Aken, Niki 70
Alba, Richard, and Philip Kasinitz 115
Alexander, Michelle 45, 53, 87
Alsop, Elizabeth 86
ambivalence 2, 3, 9, 18, 22, 100
Anderson, Paul Allen 54
Anker, Elisabeth R. 54
anti-hero 4, 5, 33, 39, 40, 44, 52, 70, 88, 107, 110, 113
anti-social 2, 3, 4–9, 13, 14, 15, 20–24, 25, 30, 3, 33–35, 37, 44, 48–49, 57–59, 63, 65–67, 70, 78, 80, 93, 95–96, 99, 103, 104, 107, 108, 109, 112, 113
anxiety 14, 15, 26, 34, 52, 64, 66, 92, 93
Armstrong, Paul B. 72
art 14, 21, 45, 51, 60–61, 63, 64, 74–75, 77–85, 86, 88, 90, 93, 94–96, 102, 109, 115
Arzheimer, Kai 11
Asim, Jabari 53
Atlas, John, and Peter Dreier 52, 54

Banet-Weiser, Sarah 27
Bannon, Sam 38
Bartlett, Bruce 27
Baudrillard, Jean 41, 78–79, 87, 88, 90, 100
Beale, James 26
Belt, Rabia 52
Bergler, Edmund 100
Bergquist, Emma D. 40
Berruz, Stephanie Rivera 71
Berryessa, Colleen, and Taylor Goodspeed 87
Betancourt, Andree 28
Biehl, Brigitte 100
Bilandzic, Helena, and Patrick Rössler 40
binge-watching 55, 58, 70, 72, 83, 100
Birke, Dorothee, and Robyn Warhol 55
Bistoen, Gregory, Stijn Vanheule, and Stef Craps 99
Blair, Tony 71
Bloodworth, James 39
Blum, Harold P. 100
Bodell, Harry 11
Bohr, Marco, et al. 38
Boltanski, Luc 87
Bonilla-Silva, Eduardo, and Austin Ashe 52
Borch III, Fred L. 73
borderline personality disorder 13–14, 18, 25, 33, 63
Borstelmann, Thomas 40
Bourdaa, Melanie 101
Bourdieu, Pierre 1, 2, 10, 80–82, 84, 85, 86, 88, 94, 102, 108–109

118 Index

bourgeois 56, 59–61, 65, 67, 69–70, 85, 95, 101
Bousquet, Marc, and Cary Nelson 11, 38
Brady-Brown, Annabel 115
Breaking Bad 1, 4, 8, 9, 12, 25, 26, 29–41, 109, 116
Brehas, Ivana 115
Brock, Maria 115
Brod, Harry 27
Broersma, Marcel, and Chris Peters 52
Brooks, David 56, 58–70, 71, 102
Brown, Jessica Autumn 53
Brown, Katherine Ann, and Todd Gitlin 51
Brown, Keffrelyn D., and Amelia Kraehe 53
Brown, Paula 39
Brunila, Kristiina 40
Brylla, Catalin 86
Bull, Sofia 87
Butler, Paul 12
Byron, Chris, and Nathan Wood 73

capitalism 8–9, 13, 15–19, 25, 26, 29, 30, 36, 48, 50, 54, 56, 60–61, 64–65, 70, 72, 79, 88, 92, 105, 107, 111
Cappella, Joseph N., and Kathleen Hall Jamieson 86
Caraley, Demetrios 51
careerism 2, 3, 6–7, 9, 42–43, 48, 50, 57, 58, 75, 104, 114
Carnes, Nicholas, and Noam Lupu 39
Carr, Anthony T. 114
Carroll, Shiloh 22
Carter, April 72
castration 18, 33, 44, 91–92, 106
Cavender, Gray 54
centrist i, 1, 3–7, 8–10, 13, 15–16, 18, 19, 21–15, 28, 32, 37, 42, 44, 48, 56–60, 64–69, 75, 77, 78–80, 83, 85, 89, 91–93, 95–99, 103–105, 107–110, 112–114
Chambers, John R., Barry R. Schlenker, and Brian Collisson 26
Charpentier, Anton 63
Chase, David 15, 25, 115
Clapton, William, and Laura J. Shepherd Constantino, Paul R., et al. 99
class conflict 19, 68
climate change 35, 90, 93, 97, 100, 101
Clinton, Bill 51, 56, 60, 65–68, 71, 76, 87
conservative 7, 9, 13, 15–17, 19, 27, 38, 43–46, 56, 65–69, 75–78, 85, 91–92, 97, 105, 106, 108, 114, 115, 116

Constantino, Paul R., et al. 38, 115
contingent faculty 11, 38
contradiction i, 6–7, 23, 60, 63, 64, 66, 79, 80, 82, 89, 91–92, 97–99, 105–107, 113
Conway, Joseph 38
Costas, Jana, and Alireza Taheri 100
Cowlishaw, Bridget Roussell 39
Crouch, Colin 54
Crozier, Gill 28
cultural capital 72
culture industry 14, 35, 43, 45, 47, 49, 51, 52, 55, 58–61, 63, 70, 77, 90, 107, 114
culture war 19, 20, 27, 42, 51, 65, 66, 106, 108
Currie, Mark 72
Currinder, Marian 52
cynicism 9, 36, 37, 52, 56, 57, 59, 63, 80, 98, 107
cynical conformity 56

Dark, Taylor E. 26
Davidson, Lindsey E. 70
Delledonne, Giacomo 70
democracy i, 5, 6, 7, 9, 12, 19, 21, 27, 30, 36, 43, 45, 54, 56, 58, 61, 65, 71, 72, 76, 77–79, 87, 104, 113–114
Democrats 16, 20, 26, 29, 32–33, 38, 47, 56, 67–68, 71, 96, 103–105, 108, 113–114
Denker, Angela 31
DePaulo, Bella 86
desire 3, 4, 7, 8, 9, 13, 14, 15, 18, 20, 21, 23, 24, 25, 29, 33, 34, 37, 43, 46, 47, 50, 57–59, 62, 65, 70, 75, 76, 80, 90–92, 95–97, 98, 99, 104, 106, 107, 111, 112
Dexter i, 1, 8, 9, 12, 70, 74–88
Deylami, Shirin, and Jonathan Havercroft 54
DiAngelo, Robin 27
Digioia, Amanda 99
DiPaolo, Marc 53
Donnelly, Colleen Elaine 100
Douthat, Ross 28
Dovi, Suzanne 72
Downes, Stephanie, and Helen Young 102
Dreier, Peter, and John Atlas 52, 54
Drew, Rob 72
drive 2, 20, 29, 33, 36, 43, 44, 58, 63, 72, 78, 85, 90, 92, 93, 96, 104, 106, 11, 114
drugs 31, 42–43, 45, 47, 53, 56, 63, 79

Echart, Pablo 40
ego-ideal 88
Ekins, Emily 27
elites 3–5, 20–21, 30–31, 54, 61, 63–64,
    68, 84–85, 98, 103, 104, 114
Ellis, Katie M. 100
Elwood, Rachel L. 100
enjoyment 2, 5, 9, 12, 13, 14, 15, 17, 20,
    21, 23, 25, 29, 31, 39, 43, 44, 46, 76,
    58, 70, 73, 81, 83, 84, 90, 92, 96, 99,
    101, 104, 106, 107, 112, 116
Enlightenment, The 5, 11, 27, 37,
    41, 53
Eschholz, Sarah, Ted Chiricos, and
    Marc Gertz 40
Evans, Tania 29

Fahy, Declan 40
Faktorovich, Anna 52
Falcone, Rino, and Cristiano
    Castelfranchi 86
Faludi, Susan 26, 100
fantasy 3, 5, 8, 9, 10, 14, 15, 18, 19,
    25, 30, 38, 42, 57–58, 85, 86, 89,
    90–94, 96–99, 100, 101, 102, 104,
    110, 112, 113
Feffer, John 71
Felski, Rita 116
Ferguson, Thomas 71
Ferreday, Debra 12
Ferrucci, Patrick 71
Ferrucci, Patrick, and Chad Painter 71
Finley, Laura, and Luigi Esposito 27
Fiorina, Morris P., Samuel J. Abrams, and
    Jeremy C. Pope 51
Fisher, Mark 10, 12, 39, 115
Florida, Richard 72
Force, William Ryan 87
Ford, Jessica, and Amy Boyle 86
Formisano, Ronald P. 26
Forrester, John 101
Foster, Hal 115
Frank, Thomas 26, 27, 72, 73, 114,
    115, 116
Fraser, Steve 115
free speech 69, 112
Freud, Sigmund 3, 7, 10, 11, 13, 14, 18,
    25, 26, 27, 28, 31, 33, 29, 40, 63, 66,
    72, 73, 78, 81, 87, 89–91, 93, 96, 99,
    100, 101, 102, 104, 106–107, 114,
    115, 116
Frumkin, R. A. 115
Fuchsman, Kenneth 101, 102
Furnham, Adrian 72

Galston, William 56
Game of Thrones, The i, 1, 4, 8, 9, 11, 85,
    89–102
Garrett, Stephen 52
Gartman, David 10
Gender 5, 10, 11, 16, 19, 26, 23, 33, 34,
    40, 42, 53, 81, 83, 85, 86, 89, 90–91,
    96, 98, 99, 100, 102, 104, 114, 115
gentrification 93–94, 101, 102
Genz, Stéphanie 99
George, Sheldon, and Derek Hook 41
Gerbner, George, et al. 40
Gething, Anna 27
Gibbs, Alan 86
Gibson III, Ernest L. 54
Giddens, Anthony 71
Giroux, Henry A. 54
Gjelsvik, Anne, and Rikke Schubart 102
globalization 102
Goldberg, Carl 101
Goldstein, Donna M., and Kira Hall 53
Gómez-Peña, Guillermo 114
Gonzales, Julia 73
Gonzalez-Sobrino, Bianca, Emma
    González-Lesser, and Matthew W.
    Hughey 51, 71
Goode, Erich, and D. Angus Vail 25
Granelli, Steven, and Jason Zenor
    12, 86
Green, Stephanie 87
Gregersdotter, Katarina, and Nicklas
    Hållén 26, 87
Gregoriou, Christiana 87
Greif, Avner 87
Grenfell, Michael, and Cheryl Hardy 88
Guastaferro, Wendy 52
Guilfoy, Kevin 39
guilt 4, 7, 9, 30, 31, 46, 58, 62, 63, 80,
    85, 90, 92–93, 96, 98, 99, 100, 104,
    107, 114

Hackett, J. Edward 71
Haney-López, Ian 53, 115
Hannell, Briony 100
Hargraves, Hunter 40
Harris, Adam 26
Harris, Geraldine 52
Harris, Marvin 102
Hartmann, Matthew 86
Harvey, Graham 99
Hassler-Forest, Dan 56
Havas, Julia, and Maria Sulimma 39
Haynes, Jo 90
Haywood, Loraine 33

HBO 1, 3, 12, 21, 24, 28, 40, 42, 51, 52, 53, 54, 59, 69, 86, 93–95, 99, 100, 101, 102, 109, 115
Hedges, Chris 2, 10, 11, 26, 38, 42, 43, 47–51, 73
Henrich, Joseph 27
Hibbing, John 116
Hirsch, Kasper 115
Hirst, Paul Q. 101
Hoel, Erik P. 114
Holladay, Holly Willson, and Melissa A. Click 11, 39
Holland, Jack 38
Holt, Robin, and Mike Zundel 52
House of Cards i, 1, 2, 8, 9, 12, 51, 55–73
Houwen, Janna 86
Hubbs-Tait, Laura, et al. 72
Hudelet, Ariane 54
humor 11, 14, 15, 25, 31, 32, 37, 39, 61, 64, 69, 105, 106, 111, 114
Huntington, Samuel P. 114
Hutcheon, Linda 10, 12, 72
Hutchinson, Darren Lenard 40, 53

id 76, 93, 101
ideology i, 1, 5–9, 16, 20–22, 24, 26, 30, 32, 35, 45, 46, 50, 56, 58, 61, 67, 70, 76, 77, 78, 80, 82, 83, 85, 89, 96, 101, 103, 113
identification 2, 3, 4, 6, 7, 14, 22, 24, 75, 76, 83, 92, 112, 113–114
individualism 4, 5–6, 7, 9, 19, 30–31, 43, 44, 57, 58, 59, 69, 75, 76, 77, 104
inequality 2, 4, 6, 10, 11, 16, 21, 22–24, 26, 28, 30, 32, 35, 38, 48, 53, 63, 64, 67, 85, 87, 95, 104, 115
irony 2, 7–10, 17, 25, 31–32, 34, 37, 39, 45, 47, 55–57, 59–65, 69, 72, 73, 79–80, 104, 105, 107–108, 110, 111, 114
Irwin, Andrew 116
Isenberg, Nancy, and Andrew Burstein 26
Izzo, Donatella 36

Jacobs, Jason 27
Jaiswal, J., C. LoSchiavo, and D. C. Perlman 53
Jameson, Frederic 26, 52, 88
Jamieson, Kathleen Hall, and Joseph N. Cappella 116
Jamieson, Patrick E., and Daniel Romer 87, 116
Jaramillo, Deborah L. 28
Jenkins, Henry 12
Jenner, Mareike 70, 72
Jöckel, Sven, and Hannah Früh 87

Johnson, Edward A., Norah Vincent, and Leah Ross 116
Johnson, Michael 12
Johnson, Paul Elliott 39
Johnston, Adrian 100
Johnston, Susan 14
Jones, Daniel Stedman 71
Jones, Patrick, and Gretchen Soderlund 72
journalism 21, 43, 46, 52, 57, 60, 71, 72
Jubin, Olivier 26

Kabaservice, Geoffrey 73
Kajtár, László 71
Kakkar, Hemant, Niro Sivanathan, and Matthias S. Gobel 102
Kantola, Anu 71
Karpf, David 28
Katz, Elihu, and David Foulkes 40
Keen, Helen 101
Keller, James R. 71
Kellner, Douglas 12, 88
Kendall, Diana Elizabeth 88
Kezar, Adrianna, and Daniel Maxey 38
Kilminster, Richard 101
Kim, Eunjoon, and Morgan Sheng 54
Kimmel, Michael, and Abby L. Ferber 39
King Lear 10, 103, 105, 113
Kitson, Janine 51
Kjeldgaard-Christiansen, Jens 39
Klarer, Mario 73
Klein, Ezra 26, 115
Knobloch-Westerwick, Silvia, Matthias R. Hastall, and Maik Rossmann 41
Kolchin, Peter 51
Kolm, Serge-Christopher 87
Kramer, Michael 73
Kubey, Robert, and Mihaly Csikszentmihalyi 53
Kulak, Önder 72

Lacan, Jacques 41, 92, 100, 101
Lanford, Daniel, and Jill Quadagno 38
Laplanche, Jean, and J. B. Pontalis 25
Lasch, Christopher 11, 34–37, 40, 46, 53, 101,
Law, Clarise S. 72
Lawrence, Regina G., and Amber E. Boydstun 102
Lazonick, William 55
Lee, David R. 12
Lee, Sang Yoon Tim, Yongseok Shin, and Donghoon Lee 38

Index **121**

Left-wing 6, 7, 11, 15–16, 19, 26, 27, 42, 46, 51, 54, 60, 65–69, 72, 73, 75, 76, 78, 85, 102, 104–105, 106, 108, 114, 115, 116
Lessl, Thomas M. 87
liberal i, 2–8, 9–10, 11, 12, 13, 15–16, 19–20, 22, 25, 26, 27, 29–31, 34–36, 38, 42–52, 58–62, 65–73, 74–79, 98, 102, 103–106, 108, 109, 114, 115
libertarian 4, 8, 10, 13, 14–16, 19, 20–22, 29, 46, 58–59, 69, 74, 77, 78, 80, 91, 103, 105, 106, 107, 109, 112–113
Liu, Alan 70
Liu, Amy 38
Lobato, Ramon 10
Locke, Jill 116
Lopez, Qiuana, and Mary Bucholtz 53
Lucks, Daniel S. 53
Luff, Jennifer 52
Lukes, Steven 11
Lyons, Siobhan 26, 116

MacDonald, Alzena 86
Mackay, Ruth 71
Macy, Anne, and Neil Terry 38
Magill, R. Jay 73
Manoliu, Ioana Alexandra 71, 72
Manza, Jeff, and Ned Crowley 73
Marsh, John 28
Martin, Brett 12, 25, 110
Marx, Karl 1, 8, 15, 26, 73, 92
masculinity 18, 19, 26, 28, 29, 30, 40, 53, 100, 114, 115
Matchett, Stephen 70
maternal super-ego 10, 14, 18, 90
Matrix, Sidneyeve 72
Mattessi, Peter 27
Maucione, Jessica 28
Maxwell, Angie, and Todd Shields 53
McAdams, Dan P. 115
McCabe, Janet, and Kim Akass 28, 101
McCahill, Michael, and Rachel Finn 54
McClary, Susan 26
McConachie, Bruce 86
McDonough, Matthew 40
McIlwraith, Robert, et al. 53
McMurran, Mary Helen 11
McNair, Brian 71
McWhorter, John 38
Mellow, Nicole 38
meritocracy 3, 21, 22, 28, 30, 38, 39, 81–82, 88, 109
metafiction 2, 32, 51, 55–59, 62–64, 71, 72, 77, 85, 89, 103, 105, 107, 114
Metcalf, Roy 72

Meyer, Matt 71
Miles, Travis 39
Miller, Brian 28
Miller, Toby 54
Milrod, David 88
Mishel, Lawrence 40
Mittell, Jason 39, 40, 54, 86
Modernity i, 5–6, 8, 9, 13, 15, 19, 22, 30, 34, 36–37, 43–45, 47, 49, 56, 58, 60, 61, 65, 74, 75–78, 87, 91, 92, 101, 104–105, 107, 108, 114
Montgomery, Martin 116
Moonves, Les 2, 21
Moore, Alfred 87
Morris, Christopher D. 100
Mosse, Hilde L. 86
Moxley Rouse, Carolyn 27
Murdoch, Rupert 10, 103, 115
Murdock, Graham 86, 102
Murphy, Jack 102
Murray, Darrin S. 11

narcissism 2, 3, 10, 11, 13, 15, 20, 21, 25, 26, 34–35, 37, 40, 44, 46, 51, 53, 54, 59–60, 62–64, 70, 73, 80, 82, 91, 92, 98–99, 101, 102, 104, 107, 108, 112, 113–114, 116
narrative 6, 9, 15, 31, 44, 53, 55, 58, 60, 70, 71, 73, 89, 90, 91–92, 94, 96, 98, 100
neoliberalism 9, 13, 25, 27, 38, 40, 54, 71, 73, 86, 109, 114, 115, 116
Netflix 58, 70, 71, 72
network television 20, 81, 83, 84, 86, 88, 93–96, 101
Newell, Walker 87
Newman, Michael Z. 10, 11, 28, 60, 88, 116
Nisbet, Robert A. 6, 11
Nisbett, Richard E., and Yuri Miyamoto
Nixon, Richard 99
Nochimson, Martha P. 25
Nodia, Ghia 54
Nurse, Angus 17, 20
Nutini, Hugo G., and Barry L. Isaac 28
Nygaard, Taylor, and Jorie Lagerwey 88

O'Brien, Benjamin Gonzalez, Loren Collingwood, and Stephen Omar El-Khatib 51
obsessive-compulsive 2–3, 5, 8, 10, 11, 15, 17, 20, 21, 25, 26, 28, 30, 44, 51, 54, 64, 72, 73, 92, 96, 99, 101, 102, 103–107, 113, 114, 115
Olivier, Bert 86

122 Index

Ostrom, Elinor 28
Ouellette, Laurie 88

Pagden, Anthony 11, 27
Parenti, Michael 12
Parmar, Inderjeet 116
Parunov, Pavao 39
Pavlac, Brian A. 99
Peeters, Carla 87
Penfold-Mounce, Ruth, David Beer, and Roger Burrows 53
Perkins, Robert L. 39
Piccinin, Fabiana, and Gabriel Steindorff 71
Pickard, Victor 10, 25
Piliawsky, Monte 51
Pilipets, Elena, and Rainer Winter 71
Pinker, Steven 36, 41, 53, 86
Pisters, Patricia 88
Pittman, Matthew, and Kim Sheehan 4
pleasure principle 7, 9, 13, 14, 15, 17, 25, 29, 31, 42, 43, 46, 47, 48, 55, 57, 58, 60, 63, 72, 75, 77, 78–80, 90, 92, 107
police 4, 43, 45–47, 49–51, 74, 75, 78,
political correctness 5, 8, 14, 15, 16, 19–20, 104, 112, 116
Pollin, Robert 72
Poniewozik, James 12, 25, 27, 79, 88, 107–108, 110–112, 115
popular culture 3, 12, 14, 16, 20, 37, 42, 47, 52, 71, 76, 84, 85, 93, 99, 103, 109, 114
Poscheschnik, Gerald 101
Posey-Maddox, Linn, Shelley McDonough Kimelberg, and Maia Cucchiara 116
Post, Jonathan Vos 102
Postman, Neil 79, 88
postmodern 10, 12, 19, 25, 85, 88, 100
Prasad, Monica, Steve G. Hoffman, and Kieran Bezila 39
prestige i, 1–8, 16, 19–25, 28, 30–31, 33, 35, 37, 40, 42–46, 48, 52, 58–63, 65, 68, 70, 74, 75, 76, 79, 80–85, 89, 90, 92, 93–96, 98, 102, 103–106, 108–110, 113–114, 115
Primo, David M. 71
profanity 8, 20, 85, 89, 90, 95, 106,
professionals 1, 7, 10, 16, 21, 29–30, 32, 43, 56–59, 60, 96, 103, 104
projection 3, 9, 35, 46, 80, 89, 93
psychoanalysis 1–3, 7–8, 10, 11, 12, 14, 18, 25, 26, 27, 41, 51, 52, 54, 63, 71, 73, 76, 88, 100, 101, 102, 103, 106, 114, 115, 116
psychopathology 1, 3, 10, 13, 15, 16, 24, 25, 35, 74, 83, 96, 97, 100, 101, 103, 113, 114,

Quinn, Roseanne Giannini 27
Qureshi, Bilal 53

race 5, 16, 19, 22, 23, 27, 28, 33–34, 40, 41, 42, 51, 52, 53, 57, 76, 81, 83, 85, 87, 98, 104, 116
racism 4, 8, 11, 26, 27, 30, 33, 38, 41, 42, 44–47, 52, 53, 57, 68, 71, 75, 115
Ragland-Sullivan, Ellie 101
Rasmussen, Mikkel Bolt 27
Rauch, Jonathan 11, 27, 52
Read, Jason 54
Reagan, Ronald 53, 87
reason 3–4, 6, 8, 14, 16, 17–18, 22, 24, 36, 41, 45, 46, 47, 51, 63, 69, 75, 76, 84, 95, 101, 103, 104, 113
Rebane, Gala 102
repression 2, 3, 4, 5, 6, 7, 8, 9, 13, 14, 15, 18, 19, 20, 21, 23, 24, 37, 38, 44, 47, 55, 58, 62, 63, 64, 66, 67, 72, 80, 90, 92, 93, 95, 96, 98, 99, 104, 106, 107, 108, 112, 115
Republicans 13, 16, 20, 29, 32–33, 42, 45, 47, 53, 56, 59, 65, 66–69, 71, 73, 78, 83, 103, 104, 106, 108, 109, 113
Ridley, Matt 27
Rifkin, Jeremy 72
Riggs, Don 101
Right-wing 4–5, 7, 8, 9, 10, 11, 14–16, 19–21, 24, 25, 26, 27, 32–24, 39, 43–49, 5, 54, 58, 58–60, 65–66, 67, 69, 73, 76, 77, 78, 79, 85, 95, 97, 100, 102, 103, 105–109, 111–114, 115, 116
Rivera, Lauren A. 11, 38, 88, 116
Roberts, Julian V., and Loretta J. Stalans 86
Roberts, Ron 26
Root, Wayne Allyn 26
Rovner, Julie 38
Ruiz, Jason 40
Ruiz, Maria Isabel Romero 11

Saltman, Kenneth J. 11
Samuels, Robert 10, 11, 12, 25, 26, 27, 28, 38, 39, 51, 52, 53, 54, 71, 72, 73, 100, 101, 102, 114, 115, 116
San Juan, Eric 39
Sandywell, Barry 88
Santo, Avi 12
Schlütz, Daniela M., Daniel Possler, and Lucas Golombek 70
Schrock, Douglas, et al. 116
Schupbach, Jillian 102
Schwabe, Claudia 99
Schwartz, Joseph M. 38
Schwartz, Stephan A. 73

science 6, 7, 19, 34, 36, 40, 45, 46, 53, 61, 65, 75, 78, 79, 80, 86, 87, 101
Senior, Jordan 26
Sennett, Richard 41
Sepinwall, Alan 12, 28
sexism 18, 30, 33, 42, 46, 68, 75, 113
shame 4, 7, 30, 62, 63, 80, 93, 101, 104, 114, 116
Shapiro, Zachary E., Elizabeth Curran, and Rachel CK Hutchinson 53
Sharland, S. 100
Shea, Brendan 12, 71
Sheehan, Helena, and Sheamus Sweeney 53
Shiller, Robert J. 116
Showtime 9, 85, 86, 87
Sienkiewicz-Charlish, Agnieszka 86
Silverman, Eric J., and Robert Arp 100
Simione, Luca, et al. 53
Singer, Irving 88
Slaughter, Matthew J. 26
slumming 5, 9, 57, 95,
Smith, Geoff, and Rahul Telang 73
Smith, Neil, and Peter Williams
Smith, Victoria L. 86, 87, 102
Snyder, Rachael 100
social status 1, 2–3, 10, 11, 22, 28, 62, 74, 85, 88, 94, 95, 102, 106, 109–110, 16
sociopathic 13, 17, 20, 29, 58, 107, 112
Sodano, Todd M. 51, 86
Soprano, Tony 2, 3, 4, 5, 8, 11, 15, 17, 20, 21, 22, 25, 26, 29, 110
Sopranos, The 1, 8, 11, 12, 13–28, 52, 109, 115, 116
Sorlin, Sandrine 70, 71
Sothern, Matthew 54
Spanò, Carmen 101
Spolander, Rebecca 59
Stankevičius, Armantas 99
Stewart, Jon 73
Stewart, Matthew 3, 10, 22–24, 28, 30, 38, 73, 102, 109, 115
Stonecash, Jeffrey M., et al. 71
streaming 1, 3, 10, 53, 58
Stubbs, Andrew 102
Succession 1, 8, 10, 99, 103–116
Sundar, Nandini 87
super-ego 8, 19, 33, 93, 100, 104, 114
surveillance 44, 51, 52, 54
survivalism 8, 29, 34
Swiech, Mark R. 54
Swirski, Peter, and Tero Eljas Vanhanen 101

Takei, Carl 87
Tally, Margaret 115
Tarly, Samwell 20

Theye, Kirsten, and Steven Melling 116
Third Way, The 56, 65–67, 71
Thompson, Kecia Driver 53
Thorburn, David 26
Thormann, Janet 101
Thorstein, and C. Wright Mills 88
Throsby, David 72
Tokgöz, Y. İ. Ğ. İ. T. 88
Toscano, Aaron A. 28
tradition 7, 8, 13, 4, 15, 16, 17, 19, 60, 66, 71, 78, 83, 91
Trejo Morales, Cristina 102
Trottier, Daniel 52
Trottier, Daniel, and David Lyon 52
Trump, Donald 2, 5, 8, 10, 11, 12, 13, 15, 17, 18, 20, 25, 26, 27, 28, 31, 39, 51, 53, 54, 73, 79–80, 88, 95, 102, 103, 106–108, 110–113, 114, 115, 116
Tsfati, Yariv, Riva Tukachinsky, and Yoram Peri 52
Tsudama, Laurena 52
Turner, Rachel 100
Tyree, Joshua M. 87

Ucan, Aylin 100
unconscious 1, 3, 7, 9, 10, 11, 12, 14, 15, 18, 19, 21, 22, 25, 29, 46, 63, 64, 73, 77, 81, 82, 85, 90, 91, 93, 101, 103, 106, 107, 112, 113, 115, 116
Underwood, Frank 2, 4, 9, 55–56, 58, 63, 65, 67, 68, 70, 71, 73
unions 4, 26, 42, 43, 48, 50, 56, 59
universities 1, 2, 3, 6, 10, 11, 16, 22, 28, 30, 38, 56, 72, 73, 43, 48, 50, 94, 109, 115
upper-middle class 1–5, 7, 9–10, 21–23, 25, 28, 29, 37, 42, 47, 48, 54, 56, 59, 62–63, 65, 67–68, 70, 74, 80–85, 93, 95, 99, 104, 108, 110, 114, 115

Verdaguer, Pierre 72
Verene, Donald Phillip 51
Vincent, Christopher J. 11
violence 4, 5, 8, 9, 14, 20, 27, 28, 33, 40, 42, 47, 49, 54, 76, 77, 78, 79, 85, 86, 87, 89, 90, 91, 95, 96, 99, 100, 106, 112
virtue signaling 2, 6, 11, 15, 30, 38, 42, 48, 58, 63, 68, 75, 96, 98, 108, 114
Voruz, Véronique, and Bogdan Wolf 101

Wake, Caroline 52
Wald, Christina 114
Walters, Ben 12
Washburn, Jennifer 72
Watts, Robert 52

Weitzer, Ronald, and Charis E. Kubrin 41
welfare state 13, 16, 17, 45, 46,
  53, 66
Wheeler, Mark 52
White, Walter 3, 4, 9, 12, 29, 31–34, 38,
  39, 40
whiteness 5, 9, 12, 15, 16, 17, 20, 23,
  26, 27, 28, 31, 32–33, 37, 39, 42, 44,
  45–46, 47, 53, 54, 57, 59, 68, 71, 74,
  83, 98, 102, 106, 110, 116
Wilk, Richard 72
Wilson, Galen 52
Wilson, Graeme John 28, 39
Wilson, Niki Caputo 26
Wilson, Rick 26
Wimberly, Cory 40

Wire, The 1, 4–5, 8, 9, 12, 25, 38, 42–54, 86
Wittwer, Preston 12
Wolfson, Todd 102
working class 2, 3, 4, 5, 6, 11, 16, 20, 21,
  32–33, 39, 40, 42, 43, 46, 47, 47, 52,
  54, 56, 59, 68, 73, 74, 83, 84, 103, 104,
  105, 106, 113

Yair, Gad 88

Zinsmeister, Karl 115
Zipes, Jack 52
Žižek, Slavoj 11, 12, 25, 39, 73, 88, 101,
  115, 116
Zuboff, Shoshana 54
Zukin, Sharon 101